In or Out?

The 60-Minute
Plain-Speaking Guide
to the
EU Referendum

C. JAMES BACON

DEDICATION

To my family

C JAMES BACON

CONTENTS

IN A NUTSHELL

The United Kingdom is one of 28 member nations in the European Union (EU). We joined in 1973, when it was known as the European Economic Community (EEC), or "Common Market".

It had come into existence with the 1957 Treaty of Rome, having six original members with France and Germany the main players. They still are, but with Germany now the leading player.

The UK joined the EEC because it was seen as a _free trade union_ in the form of reduced or zero tariffs (import duties), quotas, and trade barriers.

With the 1992 Maastricht Treaty the name was changed from EEC to EU. But it was more than a name change.

It changed from being a free trade union to a _political union_, with the aim of making most of Europe one big country (a U.S. of Europe), and one demos (people), with executive and law-making powers based in Brussels, Belgium.

But with concerns about large-scale immigration, EU regulations said to be taking over British life, evident failure in the Eurozone, and an alleged democratic 'deficit', there has been an increasing question of EU cost versus benefit.

So the government has called for a _referendum_ on 23 June, 2016, on whether the UK should remain in or leave the European Union.

C JAMES BACON

WHY THIS BOOK

The EU in or out question, whether the UK should remain in or leave the European Union (EU), is a generational game-changer that will have a big effect on all of our lives.

But with so many different beliefs, vested interests, so-called facts on both sides about the effects on jobs and the economy, and with so much rhetoric, sloganeering, empty arguments, and *especially* in an age of information overload:

> *How many of us have the time or inclination to get the real facts, sort the wheat from the chaff, and make an informed decision when the EU Referendum comes up?*

So the aim of this book is a relevant, reliable, and readable summary on *EU-In* or *EU-Out*.

As a result of intervention by the UK Electoral Commission and its aim of making things fair and square, the Referendum Question and its ballot paper will look like this:

Referendum on the United Kingdom's membership of the European Union
Vote only once by putting a cross $\boxed{\mathbf{x}}$ in the box next to your choice
Should the United Kingdom remain a member of the European Union or leave the European Union?
Remain a member of the European Union   ☐
Leave the European Union   ☐

But some of us might want to have a good look at the EU reforms Prime Minister David Cameron was able to get, and whether this might make a difference to the way we vote.

So Part I of the book includes a summary of the EU reforms aimed for, and invites you to decide whether they were "got or not".

Before this there's a discussion between three fictional characters: Ken who is EU-In, Colin who is EU-Out, and Mary, their colleague, as moderator. It's the main part of the book.

Ken   Mary   Colin

This way we get both sides of the Question, EU-In and EU-Out, side by side, with Mary keeping order and making sure all points are covered.

There is also a cost versus benefit summary where you can decide: *Are we better off in or out?*

There are a couple of other things in Part I, all of which can take about 60 minutes to read, in helping you make your own, informed decision when the EU Referendum comes up.

But you may be interested in finding out more, so Part II is offered as additional reading, and giving my own view, aiming to pack as much useful information as possible into the least number of words to make this complex subject easier to deal with.

Part III then answers three key questions that many people have.

C. James Bacon
February 2016

PART I: A 60-MINUTE READ

- Timelines: EU growth and key events

- Main views: on both sides of the EU debate

- Mary, Ken and Collin discuss EU In/Out

- EU Reforms: What the government got

- Better off In or Out? You decide

Timelines: EU growth and key events

How the EU Has Grown (1951 – 2016)

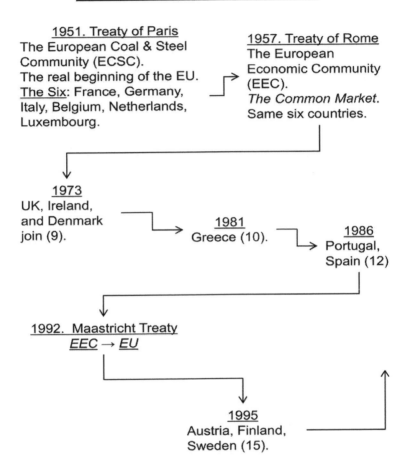

1951. Treaty of Paris
The European Coal & Steel
Community (ECSC).
The real beginning of the EU.
The Six: France, Germany,
Italy, Belgium, Netherlands,
Luxembourg.

1957. Treaty of Rome
The European
Economic Community
(EEC).
The Common Market.
Same six countries.

1973
UK, Ireland,
and Denmark
join (9).

1981
Greece (10).

1986
Portugal,
Spain (12)

1992. Maastricht Treaty
EEC → EU

1995
Austria, Finland,
Sweden (15).

How the EU Has Grown (1951 – 2016)

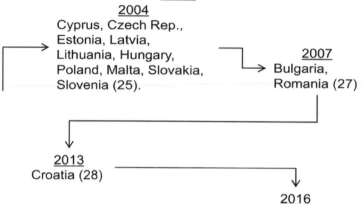

2004
Cyprus, Czech Rep., Estonia, Latvia, Lithuania, Hungary, Poland, Malta, Slovakia, Slovenia (25).

2007
Bulgaria, Romania (27)

2013
Croatia (28)

2016
Waiting to join:
Turkey, Kosovo, Albania, Macedonia, Serbia, Montenegro, Bosnia-Herzegovina. (35)

UK Proportional Influence		
1973:	1/9	11.1%
2013:	1/28	03.6%
2017?:	1/35?	02.9%

The UK presently has 73 MEPs* (9.7% out of a total of 751 MEPs), representing UK pop. of about 65 million.

*Member of European Parliament

EU Key Events (1986 – 2016)

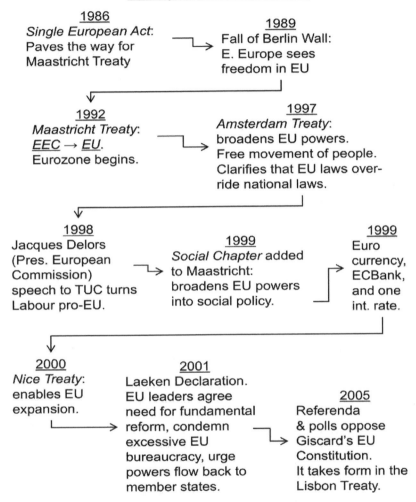

1986
Single European Act:
Paves the way for
Maastricht Treaty

1989
Fall of Berlin Wall:
E. Europe sees
freedom in EU

1992
Maastricht Treaty:
EEC → EU.
Eurozone begins.

1997
Amsterdam Treaty:
broadens EU powers.
Free movement of people.
Clarifies that EU laws over-
ride national laws.

1998
Jacques Delors
(Pres. European
Commission)
speech to TUC turns
Labour pro-EU.

1999
Social Chapter added
to Maastricht:
broadens EU powers
into social policy.

1999
Euro
currency,
ECBank,
and one
int. rate.

2000
Nice Treaty:
enables EU
expansion.

2001
Laeken Declaration.
EU leaders agree
need for fundamental
reform, condemn
excessive EU
bureaucracy, urge
powers flow back to
member states.

2005
Referenda
& polls oppose
Giscard's EU
Constitution.
It takes form in the
Lisbon Treaty.

EU Key Events (1986 – 2016)

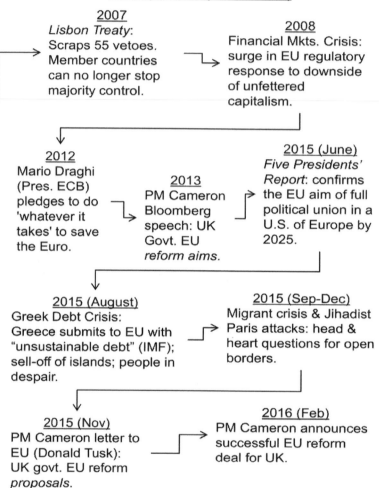

2007
Lisbon Treaty:
Scraps 55 vetoes.
Member countries
can no longer stop
majority control.

2008
Financial Mkts. Crisis:
surge in EU regulatory
response to downside
of unfettered
capitalism.

2012
Mario Draghi
(Pres. ECB)
pledges to do
'whatever it
takes' to save
the Euro.

2013
PM Cameron
Bloomberg
speech: UK
Govt. EU
reform aims.

2015 (June)
*Five Presidents'
Report*: confirms
the EU aim of full
political union in a
U.S. of Europe by
2025.

2015 (August)
Greek Debt Crisis:
Greece submits to EU with
"unsustainable debt" (IMF);
sell-off of islands; people in
despair.

2015 (Sep-Dec)
Migrant crisis & Jihadist
Paris attacks: head &
heart questions for open
borders.

2015 (Nov)
PM Cameron letter to
EU (Donald Tusk):
UK govt. EU reform
proposals.

2016 (Feb)
PM Cameron announces
successful EU reform
deal for UK.

Main views:
on both sides of the EU debate

Peace, understanding, strength, and security in one demos/people

Loss of freedom and control of borders

Being in the EU Single Market and trade bloc

The burden & cost of EU bureaucracy

The EU isn't working

Protection of workers' rights and protecting the environment

Practical economics and ordinary living

Being good Europeans

EU reform isn't going to happen

Avoiding a leap into the dark/unknown

Peace, understanding, strength, and security in one demos/people	Being in the EU Single Market and trade bloc
A vision of peace, strength understanding, security, in being one *demos,* one people, a European family, in a *United States of Europe.*	Being in the *EU Single Market* means we're virtually all one market.
This includes remaining in the EU to avoid Scotland leaving the UK.	Instead of 28 different regulations and forms for each member country we only need one; everything conforms.
And the free movement of goods, services, capital, and people across borders.	All this makes it easier and cheaper for businesses to buy and sell anywhere within the EU and expands consumer choice.
There will be a need for education to communicate the vision. On the other hand, there may be a need to limit some information.	It means a bigger market, better competition, and economies of scale.
And we need to keep the faith, work for EU reform, and remain optimistic, in staying with the vision.	And being in the *EU trade block* also gives us zero tariffs and bigger clout for getting free-trade deals in global markets.
	Outside, job losses would be in the millions.

Protection of workers' rights and protecting the environment	Being good Europeans
National governments cannot be depended on to protect workers' rights and conditions against the excesses of capitalism.	Our cultural heritage, history, language, and democracy are in Europe.
The ordinary worker needs a champion that's above national governments: the European Union.	Outside it we would be cut off, alone, isolated, and our reputation in the world diminished.
Senior executives have shown that they care more about protecting bonuses, profits, and share value than our environment.	Yet being able to travel, live, study, work, or retire in a Europe with open borders is true freedom.
The ordinary man and woman needs a champion here as well, in keeping the environment clean, safe, and healthy.	We've gained and given a lot. We invented the EU Single Market, and led the drive to open up the EU to former Soviet states.
Again, that champion is the European Union.	We must stay at the EU top table, work with our friends, and remain at the heart of a strong Europe.

Avoiding a leap Into the dark/unknown	
No-one can guarantee we would be any better off outside the European Union; that jobs would be safe; that prices and the cost of living wouldn't rise; that businesses wouldn't leave the UK. Nor can they say how long it would take and how complex to negotiate terms of leaving, or that we could negotiate a favourable free trade agreement (FTA), if an FTA could be struck at all. No-one can guarantee that we could have good access to the EU Single Market, or even survive outside the European Union. We would be worse off in every way, including higher prices in the shops and a higher cost of living. We don't need to take the risk. Remaining in the EU is the safe and less dangerous option.	

**Loss of freedom
and control of borders**

Liberty: for individual people.
Democracy: for a society.
Sovereignty: for a country's
self-governance.

It's about *freedom*, and it
continues to be taken away
from the people of the UK.

It's happening through laws
and regulations initiated by
officials in Brussels, Belgium.

They over-ride all UK laws
and all UK courts, even for the
little things in our daily lives.

And we have little control of
our own borders.

The Westminster Parliament,
Scottish Parliament, Welsh
Assembly and Northern
Ireland Assembly are all
sidelined.

We are now, in effect, largely
governed from Brussels.

The burden and cost of EU bureaucracy	The EU isn't working
The EU is far, far too big, bureaucratic, burdensome, and costly.	The Eurozone has been in decline for a decade-plus, and the IMF says its future doesn't look any better.
Many are the victims – though not always aware of who or what's behind the rules, restrictions, requirements, form-filling, and fines.	Eurozone unemployment is endemic and long-term. Spain and Greece: +20%. France, Portugal, Italy, Croatia, Cyprus: +10%. UK and Germany: 5%. The rest: 6% to 10%.
The weekly insurance that temp workers must pay, tampons being taxed as luxury items, nonsensical work rules for the NHS, are just a few examples of EU bureaucracy and officialdom.	Unemployment for young people is 50%, with young lawyers in Madrid, for example, forced to find work in London as waiters.
Many small businesses have suffered; some have been put out of business.	Growth and productivity stay stubbornly sluggish.
Brussels bureaucracy is crushing us.	The EU project just isn't working, and it makes no sense to stay tied to it.
We've got to get out from under it.	We'll be better off seeking our own destiny. There's a wider world out there.

Practical economics and ordinary living	EU reform isn't going to happen
Wages and salaries are pressed down, rents are higher, and life is harder, with EU migrant millions. Some immigration is good, when they have needed skills. But according to the Migration Observatory at Oxford University, half of new homes, including social housing, are now needed to cope with the influx. First-time buyers are unable to get on the property ladder. Economists point to the huge cost and strain on public transport, road traffic, schools, social services, the NHS, and doctors' surgeries. The EU has signalled no change, but it can't go on.	For more than 40 years the UK has tried to push for reform with the EU, but it's now clear that reform isn't going to happen. The basic problem is the *Acquis Communautaire* of the EU, in other words the body of law of the EU, which is set in stone. It's also the mind-set and vested interests of the European Commission, and the unchanging belief of European leaders in ever-closer union. And being just one of 28 countries in the EU, having less than 10% of the MEP vote, and having lost the power of veto to protect vital UK interests, there is little we can do. Reform: we've been there and tried that.

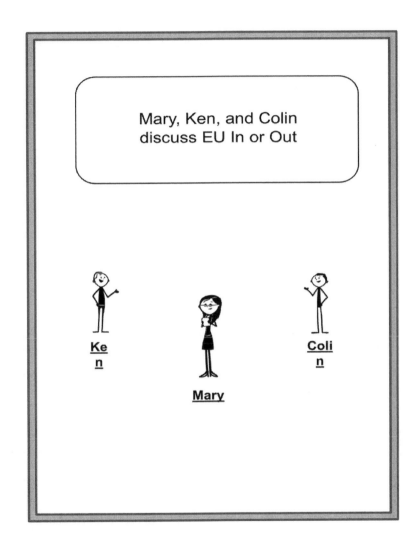

Scenario

Ken, Colin, and Mary work for a large, public services organisation with customers and clients in the government, business, and charitable sectors.

12 months ago the organisation decided to offer a service to their clients on the subject of the United Kingdom and the European Union (EU).

The motivation was simple. They wanted to assist their clients and the people who work for them with relevant, reliable, and readily accessible information on whether the UK should remain in or leave the EU, so that they might be well-equipped to make informed decisions on the Referendum when it comes up.

They selected three of their young consultants and gave them time to study the subject, giving Ken the *EU-In* role, Colin the *EU-Out* role, and Mary the job of *Moderator*.

What follows is their rehearsal before they take the show on the road.

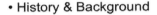

Agenda

• History & Background

• How the EU Works

• Jobs:
  - The EU Single Market
  - Foreign Direct Investment

• Immigration

• The Cost of Living

• The City & Services

• Small Businesses

OK guys, this is our agreed agenda, which we might need to amend as we go along.

We agreed EU *History & Background* is important for understanding what's going on now.

So Ken, please start us off.

Thanks Mary. It all goes back to the centuries of conflict in Europe, especially between France and Germany, and the horrors of World War I, 1914-1918.

It led many, including Picasso, Einstein, and Freud, to an utter hatred of war, and the idea of a United States of Europe to prevent war. The idea took on greater force after WWII, 1939-1945, but it was after WWI that it got started.

Arthur Salter, a British civil servant and later Oxford academic, developed a model for the idea, a *dirigiste* super-state U.S. of E. above everything and controlling everything.

The model had a commission, parliament, council of ministers, and court of justice, with the commission as the centre of authority.

But that's basically what we have today in the EU!

Clever of you to work that out, Colin.

Salter shared the model with his friend at the League of Nations, the brilliant French diplomat, ace-networker, and master manipulator Jean Monnet. He took the model and ran with it.

He convinced senior European politicians, such as Robert Schuman when he was French Foreign Minister, to adopt Salter's model.

So this whole European Union started with one man's academic model putting feet on an idea, and another man's pushy and persuasive personality?

Well, a lot of other things had to happen but yes, you could put it that way.

Sorry guys, just one little thing before we go much further on this EU In or Out question.

I'm sure we're agreed that what we're discussing is a hugely important issue for our generation and generations to come.

So our job here, and the solution we aim to provide, is to deliver *useful information* on both sides of the question.

We want to make it easier for our customers to make an informed decision, on whether to remain in or leave the EU.

This means we *don't* want to be giving any rubbish, rhetoric, false facts, hostilities, or be interrupting, or grandstanding. And please try to control the passions, fellas.

We want to make it better than a typical TV type of debate.

Are we agreed?

Thanks Mary, yes I agree.

But Ken, you've left out the *real* reason why French leader *General De Gaulle* said NO, twice, to UK entry to the EEC.

It was because he needed to get the Common Agricultural Policy and its subsidy arrangements in place for French farmers.

And this was because (a) French farmers had a big presence in the National Assembly, (b) there was a strong Communist party in France, and (c) the Fourth Republic's position was precarious. So De Gaulle had to deliver something big.

Also, if it hadn't been for *Paul-Henri Spaak* the EU might not have happened.

Then *Altiero Spinelli* , another big personality, took over to make Maastricht happen.

This whole thing is built on conspiracy, deception, and big personalities!

Yes, thanks Mary, I also agree.

But Colin, don't you know that *all* politics is about conspiracy, deception, and big personalities?

Alright, but you didn't mention that in joining the EEC in 1973 we were forced to give up our ties to the Commonwealth family. Although joining *was* very successful in forcing us to buy French butter and beef!

Another big cost was and is the huge amount of money we give for the Common Agricultural Policy (CAP) to protect French farmers.

And a very, very big cost was the loss of UK fishing grounds on being forced to give them up under the EU's Common Fisheries Policy (CFP) in 1973.

It removed a *huge* part of our natural resources and wealth, and destroyed the livelihoods of *tens of thousands* of Scottish, English, Welsh, and N. Irish fishermen.

Mary, could I show the pre-EEC UK fisheries map?

Just a minute Colin, the CAP is now about one-third of the EU Budget.

And UK farmers get back about £3 billion CAP money every year.

Also, the CFP was reformed in 2014 and is now a lot fairer and sustainable.

Right Mary, I'm happy to see Colin's fisheries map.

Well Ken, I'm not exactly sure what it is Colin wants to show, and it might not be very relevant.

But go ahead Colin, I'm curious to see this.

I suggest it's relevant, Mary, because it gives an idea of what we could get back in fishing wealth if we leave the EU. It is or was the largest fishing grounds in the EEC.

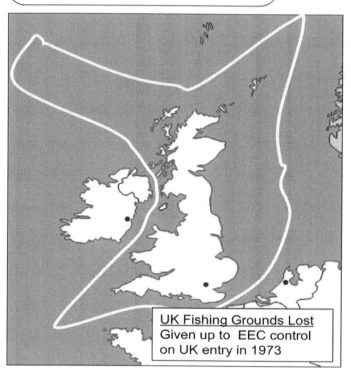

UK Fishing Grounds Lost
Given up to EEC control
on UK entry in 1973

OK Colin, I regret that loss, but it was a UK government decision at the time.

However, the ECSC, EEC, and EU has stopped France Germany, or anyone else starting another war. It got the Nobel Peace Prize in 2001.

Colin, you're missing a fundamental point.
The EU is about European unity, being one people. That's how you prevent war.

A United States of Europe will make us all one *demos*, one people, one family.

Collectively we can make a better world. It's what we need more than ever.

But the threat of war after WWII was from Soviet expansionism, with strong communist parties in France, Italy, and Greece. It wasn't any threat from Germany starting war.

Germany was looking for redemption. France wanted to protect its small farmers. So the two countries became lovers and got married.

De Gaulle and Adenaur signed the Élysée Treaty in 1963, and it began the French-German leadership of the EEC or EU.

But since 1949 the real peace-keeper in Europe has not been the ECSC, EEC or the EU.

It has been NATO, and it has worked out well for peace & security.

Just to come in quickly guys,
this is fascinating stuff!

Colin, I thought we agreed no rhetoric and
just giving our customers useful
information? So what's this rubbish about
France and Germany becoming lovers and
getting married?

On the other hand, let's agree that:
- if you want to peer into the future,
- you've got to understand the present,
- and to understand the present,
  you've got to know the past.

So what we're doing here is useful.
Keep going fellas!

Thanks Mary.
But Colin, you're missing something else. You know that a government must defend its citizens from external threat. So to tackle terrorism and jihadist attacks we have to share and coordinate data, police, and justice.

For this we've got to stand with our European friends and be part of Europe.

Ken, the EU's Schengen Information System (SIS) allows sharing of data on crime and terrorism.

But this could be done through *Interpol*, the *international* police organisation which has been handling this kind of thing successfully since 1923.

Your point being?

We don't need to be in the EU to share and coordinate data, have extradition treaties, and so forth. The EU isn't really needed.

The reason I give *Interpol* as an example is that it's *inter*-governmental, not *supra*-governmental like the EU.

Inter-government or *inter*-national means *willing* and *voluntary* co-operation between countries. *Supra*-government or *supra*-national means *above* national governments.

Agenda

✓ History & Background

✓ The Nature of the EU

How the EU Works

▪ Jobs:
  - The EU Single Market
  - Foreign Direct Investment

▪ Immigration

▪ The Cost of Living

▪ The City & Services

Hold on, please, gentlemen.
It's important to know the *nature* or character of anything or anyone with whom we're involved.

It seems you've flowed into the *nature* of the European Union and what it should or shouldn't be doing. But that's OK.

So please carry on, and think we'd better add *The Nature of the EU* to our Agenda.

OK Mary, no problem.

I see what you mean Colin, but here's the difference:
the European Union is a *family* of nations with a clear need for central direction, co-ordination, and control.

It has to have this so as to actually achieve things and get things done, to improve prosperity, quality of life, and give strength, unity, and security across the European family.

As a current example, the European Arrest Warrant (EAW) enables us to stand together against terrorists and jihadists. We can arrest them in one country and send them to another where they're wanted for terrorist acts.

I'm glad you mentioned the EAW Ken, because it's an example of the European Commission using an excuse to extend its powers.

Let's say you're in Bucharest, capital of Romania, on holiday. You're seen talking to a well-known drug dealer who has approached you. You then get back home and find the police at your door. You're being sent back to Bucharest on suspicion of drug dealing. There's nothing UK authorities can do about it.

That's how the EAW works. EU authority over-rides UK authority.

Look Colin, you're using an extreme and unlikely example there.

All international law over-rides national law, and if a country agrees to abide by an international law, then it's not a matter of being over-ridden.

Alright Ken, we'll agree to disagree on that; I believe it's a very possible example. But the thing is the EAW should be an *inter*-government thing, like extradition, not a *supra*-government thing.

I'd like to ask Mary if I can put something up on the screen.

Mary, it's important we clarify the fundamental difference between two very different things:
    supra-governmental versus
      inter-governmental.

Can I show this?

Well, this could be interesting. I'd love to know what *supra* is supposed to mean, and how it's relevant, so it's OK with me.

Just a minute Ken. Can I say it's fascinating, listening to you and Colin discuss these things.

You both have more in common than you might think. I'm sure prosperity, quality of life, strength, unity, and security are very important to both of you. It's just that you have different ways and ideas for achieving these things.

The EAW, for example, it depends how you look at it. You're both obviously against terrorism, and one of you sees the EAW as an example of essential European cooperation in this horrible, modern war. The other sees the EAW as a power taken over and exercised by the EU.

But that's people; we're all different.

OK Colin, I'm going to trust you on this *supra* thing being important.

> The EU is an extra layer of government on top of our national government.

Supra- Governmental	*Inter-* Governmental
Above nations and national governments	Between nations and national governments
Control over national governments	Co-operation between national governments
Over-riding national laws	Respecting national laws
Centralised planning/control	De-centralised planning/control
Appointed PM/President, and cabinet/executive	Elected PM and cabinet.
Big government	Devolved government
Imposed government	Self/sovereign govt.
Autocracy/bureaucracy	Democracy
Exemplars: *Global Organisations*	
The European Union	NATO, UN, G20, WTO, WHO, Basel Committee, ISO, IEA, IMF, OECD, the Commonwealth.
Exemplars: *Countries*	
The former Soviet Union.	Switzerland.

You're coming on too strong Colin, comparing the European Union with the Soviet Union.

EU member nations are able to meet in the EU parliament, Council of Ministers, or European Council. Also, each national government appoints its European Commissioner.

Ken, if EU/USSR seems too strong a comparison, I'm not the first to say it.

So tell me, what do you think of the EU ignoring the people's NO vote against the Lisbon Treaty in Ireland, France, Denmark and The Netherlands?

Wasn't that autocratic?

However, you brought up the EU parliament, and we have *How the EU Works* as an Agenda item. Lets wait 'til we get to that.

Right, I'm going to ask for equal time to give the Europe viewpoint. It's the Schuman Declaration, which Jean Monnet wrote for Robert Schuman, French Foreign Minister.

It was the founding document of the EU, 9th May, 1950, the EU's national day.

OK, here's the founding document of the ECSC, EEC, and EU.

The Schuman Declaration (abbreviated)

World peace cannot be safeguarded without efforts proportionate to the dangers which threaten it. The contribution an organized Europe can bring to civilization is indispensable to the maintenance of peaceful relations. But it will not be made all at once. It will be built through achievements for a de facto solidarity.

The coming together of the nations of Europe requires that Franco-German production of coal and steel be placed under a common High Authority, within an organization open to the other countries of Europe. The solidarity in production will make it plain that any war between France and Germany becomes not merely unthinkable, but materially impossible. This will be offered to the world with the aim of contributing to raising living standards and promoting peaceful achievements.

The movement of coal and steel between member countries will be free from customs duty, and conditions will gradually be created to provide for the more rational distribution of production.

The common High Authority entrusted with the management of the scheme will be composed of independent persons appointed by the governments. High Authority decisions will also be enforceable in other member countries.

Ken, this *High Authority* in the Schuman Declaration; I assume this is the European Commission; correct?

Absolutely correct.
But can I come back to your comment about the Commonwealth. In the first place I'm not sure what it actually does.

In the second place, the Commonwealth doesn't have nitty-gritty things to do like the EU does.

In the third place, the Commonwealth is too remote to us, whereas other EU member countries are our next door neighbours.

In the fourth place, as far as the EU is concerned, there cannot be vetoes to protect what are often selfish national interests. If there were, the EU would never get anything done.

You're right Ken.
We don't really know what the Commonwealth does.

The EU's PR in our schools, even down to infants, is way ahead.

But the Commonwealth isn't remote at all. We live in a global village now. Christchurch UK and Christchurch New Zealand are Internet seconds apart.

And yours is the EU view.

For self-governing nations, it's different.

It seems what we're coming down to is one person looking at a set of facts, and another person looking at the same facts, and the two coming up with different conclusions.

So Ken, you see the EU as a family of nations.

Colin, you see the EU as a bit like the former Soviet Union or USSR.

I wish we could use the Socratic Method of question and answer to flesh out what you really think and why you think it.

But we're doing ok.

Thanks Mary.

Also Colin, if we're not in the EU family it means we're not in Europe. We're cut off.

It's like we've pulled up the drawbridge and retreated from the world.

I wish you wouldn't call the EU *Europe*. The EU is not *Europe* and Europe is not the EU.

We wouldn't be cut off from Europe, but we would be out of a U.S. of E. super-state.

So Ken, please don't say the EU is *Europe*!

OK, keep your shirt on. But the EU and Europe *are* practically the same.

And c'mon, we *will* be cut off, from Europe and the World. We'll just be Little Englanders, trying to hang on to the Old Empire, and stuck in the middle of the Atlantic.

We'll be economic and political minnows.

Ken, let me suggest the difference between us. You're *Europeanist*, whereas I'm *Internationalist*.

Like Winston Churchill, if I might use the example, I see us being part of *more than Europe*, even though Europe is very important to us.

So leaving the EU as you'd like us to do, leaving the world's third biggest trading block; are you seriously saying we'd be better off?

Colin I wouldn't compare the UK with Switzerland if I were you. They pay big money to have access to the EU Single Market.

As for the Commonwealth, you're still stuck in the past. If there really were trade opportunities with the Commonwealth they would have happened by now.

Ken, we have the fifth biggest economy in the world.

Not being shackled to the EU we'd be free to trade on our own merit and cut trade deals, like for example Switzerland and other countries do very successfully with much bigger countries like China, Japan, and India. We'd be free to do free trade!

As for the *Commonwealth*; a massive opportunity for trade!

There'd be some truth in that Ken, if it we weren't barred from making trade deals with the Commonwealth.

And we don't have a seat on the World Trade Organisation (WTO), like Switzerland does. The EU has it.

The WTO *really is* a top table, but we can't have a seat on it as long as we're in the EU!

Just a minute guys, we seem to be going off topic.

We were on *EU History & Background*, then we got into *The Nature of the EU*.

Now you've started getting into trade, which we'll get to shortly in connection with jobs.

And Ken, let's not have that rhetoric on "Little Englanders", "being stuck in the past", and "stuck in the middle of the Atlantic", "pulling up the drawbridge and retreating from the world."

It's not the kind of spirit we want. Remember, our customers are looking for *useful information*.

I liked where we were on the EU preventing war and being good for peace and understanding, so Colin, let's see you pick up and help us finish on that.

OK, thanks Mary.

Look Ken, if the EU is good for peace and understanding, what about the UN, UNESCO, UNICEF, and other international organisations? Do we really need the EU?

What concerns me is a big, all-powerful EU super-state in Brussels with:

- A very well paid, very large, bureaucratic, unelected, yet all-powerful *European Commission* that initiates and controls all EU law-making.
- An *EU Parliament* with MEPs whose job is to simply give the nod to EU laws that over-ride UK laws.
- A *European Court of Justice*, which arbitrates and over-rides UK courts.
- An executive cabinet in its *Five Presidents* . . .

. . . Colin, you've forgotten what Mary said about going on for too long . . .

. . . but none of these things have happened without being agreed by a UK government.

Let me show you the checks and balances: how the Parliament works, in its *Ordinary Legislative Procedure*.

- . . . Its own 500 million EU "citizens" carrying EU passports and driving licenses – we lost our British ones.
- An EU diplomatic and foreign affairs service in the *European External Action Service*, with delegations in about 140 countries displacing our own diplomatic embassies.
- An EU national flag and anthem.
- An EU currency (the Euro) and Bank.
- An EU *Committee of the Regions...*

Agenda

✓ History & Background

✓ The Nature of the EU

✓ How the EU Works

- Jobs:
  - The EU Single Market
  - Foreign Direct Investment

- Immigration

Hang on Ken, it looks like you're taking us from the Nature of the EU into *How the EU Works.*

It's no problem, but again there seems to be a bit of antipathy creeping in between you guys. Let's try to have a bit more *amicability*, if possible.

Let's keep in mind what Voltaire, the French philosopher, said:
I do not agree with what you have to say but I'll defend to the death your right to say it.

OK Ken, let's see how your EU Parliament works.

How the EU Parliament Works
Does not show 'Comitology'

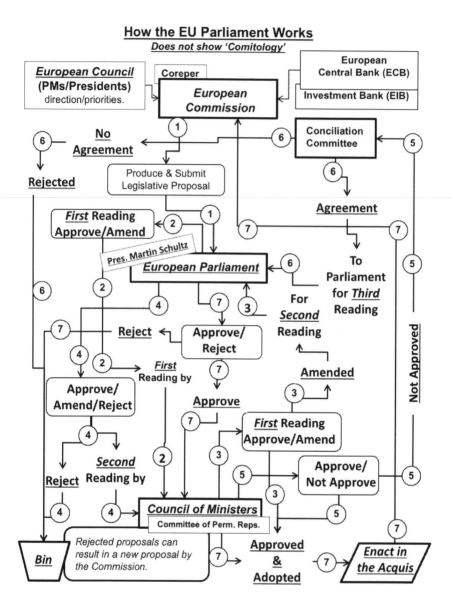

Follow the numbers, and you'll see the balance: *Commission, Parliament,* and *Council of Ministers.*

And the process in the UK Parliament at Westminster is almost as complicated.

As for *Comitology*, it's the discussion and horse-trading that takes place in hundreds of committees and interest groups before report-backs to Parliament.

Parliament votes on the outcome of the Comitology process. And as you know, the European Parliament is democratically elected.

We need a health warning with that Ken! And what does "Comitology" mean ?

Sorry but there's no balance at all. The Commission is in charge. If the Europe Parliament rejects something the Commission can simply re-word it and send it back. You can't win against the Commission.

I'm told that, with all EU legislation:
a. The Commission initiates it.
b. Parliament tweaks and rubber-stamps it.
c. Council of Ministers approves it.

There's no real debate.

The Commission doesn't so much initiate, it *proposes.*

And all the real debate happens before it gets to Parliament.

But the *European Commission* and Pres. Juncker run the show, supported by the Committee of Permanent Reps or *Coreper*.

Coreper controls the agendas and terms of reference for the committees and working parties.

They're unelected Brussels bureaucrats not accountable to anyone, but controlling our lives.

The Commission and Coreper run the show, but on behalf of national governments.

We vote for our MEPs, and *they* control the European Commission.

And the Commission *is* accountable. It can be *removed* by the European Parliament.

C'mon Ken, removal isn't going to happen.

And with 73 UK MEPs out of 751 that gives the UK 9.7% of the Parliament, which doesn't give us much of a say at your top table, does it?

Also, each UK MEP represents nearly a million people. How can an MEP really represent you?

So Ken, we've seen that the Commission manages all EU legislation, policies, budgets, funding, and agendas.

And our 73 MEPs have an incredible volume of legislation and very wordy, very complex, obscurantist *Eurospeak* from the Commission.

This is one of the ways the Commission gets its way and by-passes the democratic process, through information and obfuscation overload!

That's nonsense Colin. The European Parliament has a lot of regulations to go through, but our MEPs have ample opportunity to give their views, not just in the Parliament but in the committees and working parties.

I don't think so Ken, our MEPs don't get ample opportunity, not really.

In the EU Parliament legislation just gets steamrollered through without proper debate.
MEPs are expected to just give the nod, and they do.

Also, the Commons European Scrutiny Committee in our UK Parliament get to comment, with just eight weeks to do it, but it has no power to change anything.

And Ken; Commission President Jean-Claude Juncker is virtually the EU P.M. But I don't remember voting for him!

Allow me to correct you there, Colin. The President of the European Commission is appointed by national governments who are democratically elected.

Look Ken, in the UK, if we don't like the sons of bachelors we can vote them out, but it's very difficult to get rid of the European Commission or its President.

Don't you remember our PM David Cameron objecting strongly to the appointment of Jean-Claude Juncker. but being over-ruled by Angela Merkel, the German leader?

OK guys I think we've had enough of how the EU works, at least in the EU Parliament and with the European Commission.

Colin, *sons of bachelors*? I've not heard that one before.

But the other thing is these fancy words you use: *obfuscation* and *obscurantist*.

Some people might not be clear about what you mean.

It's language that's unclear, theoretical, and confusing, even deliberately so. *EuroSpeak* is sometimes said to be this kind of language, used by EU *technocrats*, as they like to be called.

So can I ask you to try to keep to the KISS principle: Keep It simple stupid!

But Ken, tell us what the *Acquis* is, referred to in the bottom-right corner of *How the EU Parliament Works*.
It's important isn't it?

Sure Mary, its full name is the Acquis Communautaire. It's the body of EU law and set of powers *acquired* by the EU.

It represents all the treaties, protocols, decisions, directives, regulations, and powers or *competences*, of the EU.

It's the EU bible. It's been agreed, and it's set in stone.

So if the *Acquis* or body of law is set in stone, doesn't that say something about EU reform?

It takes all 28 member countries to agree if you want to change anything.

And then you need approval of the EU Parliament and Council of Ministers.

And you've also got the European Court of Justice to worry about. They *always* support the Commission, the ever-growing *power* of the Commission, and the EU goal of *ever-closer union*.

OK, let me stop you again there guys.

Like I said before, we're getting some good discussion here.

But I think we need to finish up how the EU *works*.

Ken, can you now help us finish on this by giving us some idea of how the EU is *organised*?

We've got to move on.

Sure Mary, I can show you a *simplified*
version of how the EU is organised.

It's only the main connections that are
shown, by arrows. It would be too
complicated to show them all.

I'll also show you some of the buildings
for the main EU committees and
agencies, but excluding the EU
parliamentary committees and all the less
important EU agencies and committees.

The pictures are just to give you a picture
of things and make it all real.

After this, I think you'll have a fairly good
understanding of the how the EU works
and how it's organised.

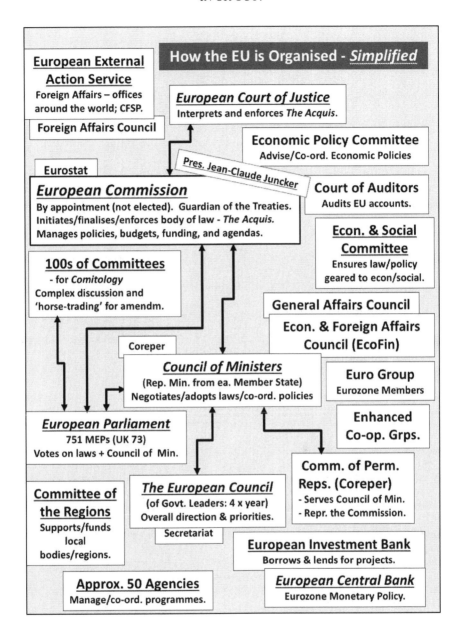

How the EU is Organised - *Simplified*

European External Action Service
Foreign Affairs – offices around the world; CFSP.

Foreign Affairs Council

European Court of Justice
Interprets and enforces *The Acquis*.

Economic Policy Committee
Advise/Co-ord. Economic Policies

Eurostat

Pres. Jean-Claude Juncker

European Commission
By appointment (not elected). Guardian of the Treaties.
Initiates/finalises/enforces body of law - *The Acquis*.
Manages policies, budgets, funding, and agendas.

Court of Auditors
Audits EU accounts.

Econ. & Social Committee
Ensures law/policy geared to econ/social.

100s of Committees
- for *Comitology*
Complex discussion and 'horse-trading' for amendm.

General Affairs Council

Econ. & Foreign Affairs Council (EcoFin)

Coreper

Council of Ministers
(Rep. Min. from ea. Member State)
Negotiates/adopts laws/co-ord. policies

Euro Group
Eurozone Members

European Parliament
751 MEPs (UK 73)
Votes on laws + Council of Min.

Enhanced Co-op. Grps.

Committee of the Regions
Supports/funds local bodies/regions.

The European Council
(of Govt. Leaders: 4 x year)
Overall direction & priorities.

Secretariat

Comm. of Perm. Reps. (Coreper)
- Serves Council of Min.
- Repr. the Commission.

European Investment Bank
Borrows & lends for projects.

Approx. 50 Agencies
Manage/co-ord. programmes.

European Central Bank
Eurozone Monetary Policy.

European Court of Justice

European Commission (approx. 35,000 staff)

EU Parliament, Brussels

Alternate Parliament, Strasbourg

European External Action Service
Embassies in 140 countries

Economic & Social Committee

Office of EU President

Committee of the Regions

Institute of Energy & Transport

Economic Policy Committee.

Council of Ministers

European Council

European Investment Bank   European Central Bank

Ken, let me ask you:
The alternate Parliament in
Strasbourg; is that the one that
makes the European 751-
member EU Parliament plus
about 2,000 staff take a five-
hour return train journey each
month from Brussels in
Belgium to Strasbourg in
France?

Doesn't it symbolise the EU
waste we have to pay for?

Ah, so you know about
Strasbourg? That's
something we agree on.

The EU Parliament has
tried to stop the waste of
money on this monthly jaunt
but, unfortunately,
has failed thus far.

This is a reform that
everyone is agreed on
except the French
leadership, so I'm sure
it'll happen eventually.

Sorry Ken, but again,
doesn't that say
something about
hopes for EU reform?

If you can't get reform
on something like that,
what *can* you get
reform on?

Now do you
understand why PM
David Cameron didn't
have a hope in trying
to get EU reforms?

As I say, we're still
fighting for reform, and
it's a reason for staying
with the EU.

After all, you can't
reform something if you
don't stay with it.

Agenda

✓ History & Background
✓ The Nature of the EU
✓ How the EU Works

✓ *Jobs*:
  - The EU Single Market
  - Foreign Direct Investment

Immigration

The Cost of Living

The City & Services

Small Businesses

Let me stop you there guys.

It's time we got on to *Jobs*,
starting with *The EU Single Market*.

First, it'll become easier if we clarify what the options are on the EU Single Market:

1. Remaining in the EU and Single Market as is.

2. Leaving the EU and still having access to the Single Market through a *FTA*, so:
   (a) not having to pay EU protective import tariffs on things we import from *inside* the *EU.*
   (b) not having to pay EU protective import tariffs on things we import from *outside* the EU (since we're no longer a member of the EU).
   (c) possibly consulted on Single Market standards.

3. Leaving the EU and still having access but *not* having an FTA, so:
   (a) facing EU protective import tariffs.
   (b) not having to pay EU protective import tariffs on things we import from *outside* the EU.
   (c) not consulted on Single Market standards.

So membership of the EU is not needed for access to the EU Single Market.

But before we get into the EU Single Market, do we have any comments on the job losses in steel?

Yes, well, the big job losses in Port Talbot, in Sheffield, and other parts of the UK, are mostly due to the downturn in the Chinese economy, and cheap Chinese steel being dumped on world markets, making UK steel non-competitive.

But steel-making takes a lot of energy in turning raw iron into molten steel, so high electricity prices are also a factor, again making us uncompetitive.

I don't think the UK government is helping much, with the way they've been cosying up to the Chinese. And they don't seem to be doing much to bring energy prices under control.

Ken, neither of us want to make political capital out of communities being devastated by job losses like these.

The dumping of cheap steel by the Chinese is against WTO rules, on which the UK's seat is taken by the EU.

The UK doesn't have power to influence the WTO on this.

Same with energy prices under EU energy policies, and complex tie-in with EU climate targets.

It's Brussels you need to be looking to on this.

OK, let's stop there, and let's hope and pray that something useful and practical might be done about those job losses in South Wales, Sheffield, and other places.

And that the people and their communities might even come out stronger than before, with better opportunities to replace the loss of those steel jobs.

But we have to get back to the EU Question.

Ken, could you please get us going on Jobs and the EU Single Market.

OK Mary, well yes, the EU Single Market certainly has big benefits for jobs and employment.

Before the EU, the *EEC* was about *free trade*; free of import tariffs, duties, and quotas.

That's why the UK joined the EEC under PM Edward Heath in 1973, to be part of what was usually called the *Common* Market.
It was later, in the 1980s, that it evolved into a *Single* Market.

Could I clarify something based on what Mary said. We *don't* need to be in the EU to have access to the Single Market. A lot of countries outside the EU, like for example the USA, have this situation.

We may not be consulted on EU standards or regs, but it's not a problem when they often come from global bodies such as WTO, UNECE, ISO, the Basel Committee on banking, or Codex Alimentarius for international food standards.

Also, if we have a free trade agreement with the EU, and being an important customer, like Norway, we'd likely be consulted. If not, we'd be like a lot of other countries who export into the EU.

Just a minute Ken, before either of you get too much into the benefits of the EU Single Market,

Or whether we need to be in the EU to fully enjoy its Single Market benefits.

We need to clarify what the Single Market itself is all about.

Are you going to tell us about that?

Sure, Mary.
The EU Single Market is about making regulations and standards for products and services the same across the EU.

It's one, big market.

It's good for jobs, because the Single Market opens up bigger markets to UK businesses, plus it gives greater competition, plus it lowers unit costs, plus it means wider consumer choice.

It simply makes it a lot easier to trade.

Can I respond?
First, the *UN Economic Commission for Europe* (UNECE), promotes European economic integration across Europe in policy dialogue, negotiation of legal forms, development of regulations, and exchange of best practice.

In other words, UNECE is about making regulations and standards the same across the EU.

Second, the *World Trade Organisation* (WTO) is pushing the same thing globally.

Neither of these organisations are *supra*-governmental, or cost us *mega*-bucks, or have the PR and recognition of the EU. But they do the same single-market thing.

The EU is increasingly a middleman.

OK, we can look at your Lord thing, but a single market needs rules, and the EU Single Market has just one set of rules, instead of 28.

However, the Commission launched a *better regulation* drive in 2012 to reduce bureaucracy, and we have a *Commissioner* overseeing the issue.

Right Colin, with Mary's permission, let's see what Lord whoever-he-is said on bureaucracy!

But the benefits of a single market, EU or not, is one thing on which we're agreed.

What concerns me , Ken, is the cost side of the EU Single Market; the bureaucracy burden.

Multinationals are better able to handle this, compared to small businesses.
They have the resources and power, and often an office in Brussels, to lobby the European Commission.

But EU regs are forced on all of us, *across the whole economy,* exporting or not.
It's a *huge* added cost for the NHS, local councils, govt. departments, clubs, pubs, hairdressers, and sole traders, when they don't do any exports!

Can I show you what Lord Acton said about bureaucracy?

The Single Market includes most of Europe. Norway, Switzerland, and Lichtenstein aren't in the EU but have access to the Single Market.
The Balkan States are waiting to join the EU, so is Turkey.
Belarus, Ukraine, and Moldova aren't in the EU. All of the white part is one, big, Single Market!

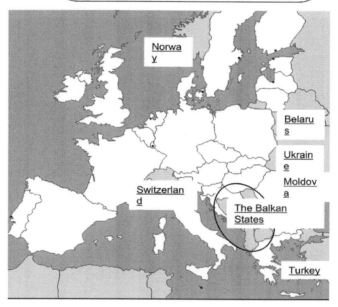

I'm showing this because EU bureaucracy:
(a) Is underplayed, unseen, un-costed.
(b) Just calling it "red tape" doesn't do it,
(c) EU bureaucracy makes life hard.

Bureacracy, or the interference of a centralised government in matters of family and individual life, is a natural growth from the supposed needs and expediency of The State.

The great characteristic of true bureaucracy is the intimate conviction of its conductors that the provisions made by them cover the whole area of human life and thought.

Hence the intolerant, monopolising, intrusive character of all true bureaucracy.

It can arise gradually under every form of policy, and renders every form of government despotic.

Its only aim is perpetually to discover new modes of interference, provide more work for the bureau, and subject the people ever more completely to its will.

Its power does not reside in any one person but in the system.

From: *Essays in the History of Liberty.*
John Dalberg-Acton (Lord Acton)

If that's supposed to refer to EU bureaucracy I disagree.

The European Commission is pro-active in proposing rules and regulations for health and safety, the environment, climate change, worker's rights, justice and home affairs, social needs...

The Working Time Directive is a good example.

It's mainly about workers not being *made* to work more than 48 hours per week.

OK Ken, if it's necessary to be pro-active in a particular area why can't our own UK Government be pro-active, in *co-operation* with other governments if needed.

The difference is we'd be co-operating *voluntarily* with other countries, not compelled by unelected Brussels bureaucrats.

Pope Francis, on a visit to the EU Parliament at its Strasbourg home in 2014, warned that "bureaucracy is crushing Europe".

And democracy is at risk from "unseen empires".

C'mon Colin, nobody is forcing anything on anyone. The EU is all about co-operation based on treaties that have been signed up to.

Now Mary, It's my turn to show something.

I'm sharing this excerpt from an article because it shows the EU is doing something about it.

I have changed the EU EurActiv.com. 29 Sep. 2014. Edmund Stoiber was the EU's Mr Red Tape. Retiring after seven years he said: *"It is too bureaucratic."*

"…Finallly the EU is beginning to understand that not everything can be nor must be regulated", he said.

Commissioner Frans Timmermans can now issue a veto if a regulation is considered excessive.

Stoiber said: *"The EU should require itself and its member states to reduce bureaucratic red tape by 10% over the next two years. This should not only apply to the EU, but equally to national governments."*

"Small-and medium-sized enterprises suffer the most from Red Tape," Stoiber said.

"The EU should not concern itself with bans on high-heels for hairstylists or the composition of Neapolitan pizzas."

"The necessity of cutting bureaucratic red-tape is now on the minds of EU politicians. That was my goal," Stoiber said.

OK Ken, so Mr EU Red Tape, (who is a German, and Germans have a good reputation for efficiency,) did some good work.

But getting back to the Working Time Directive, which the UK strongly objected to when we were out-voted on it, it's ill thought out, clumsy, and said to be costing the NHS millions annually in extra staffing.

But even that isn't the main point. The main point is this:

Whether it's a good thing or bad, what right does Brussels have to tell us how to run our lives and our country?

Can't we govern ourselves?

Firstly Colin, we accept things like the WTD because we're in the EU Single Market and we're also signed-up members of the EU Social Chapter, which was annexed to the Maastricht Treaty.

Second, it's about protection of workers' rights and health. I'm sure you'll agree that long hours, the main thing covered, aren't good for your health.

Third, if one country in the EU achieves competitive advantage by allowing sweat shops and very long hours, then that's an unfair advantage. By disallowing this kind of thing the EU creates a level playing field.

There might be another problem, Colin. If you're coming from outside the Single Market you might find the goods detained until there's evidence they conform with EU standards.

Customs Officers will be asking: "Where are your EU certificates?" If you don't have the ones they like it'll be "Sorry, we don't recognise these."

If Customs Officers were to do that kind of thing, they'd be in trouble. It would be discrimination, and against not only WTO but EU rules as well.

And remember, the UK is the EU's biggest customer, so it'll be in the interests of EU companies to have a EU/UK free trade agreement, or FTA.

And quickly.

You're assuming, Colin, that negotiating a FTA would be quick and easy, and that the UK would get what it wants.

Ken, there are EU FTAs with 27 other countries. Why shouldn't *we* have a good FTA with the EU?

But Ken, can I point to one big concern about the EU Single Market.

It's whole emphasis is on regulations and standards for the production, distribution, and export of *physical products*, as opposed to *services*, which is fine for countries such as Germany and France with their emphasis on physical products.

But for a country like the UK with its diverse economy and a global strength in *services*, it's not good.

The EU has been backward in coming forward to open up the Single Market for services.

So the *net effect* for the UK is that the EU Single Market, with its regulatory bureaucracy extending to the *whole* of the UK economy, is *negative*!

OK Colin, that's a good reason why we should remain in the EU, to fight for the extension of the EU Single Market to services.

The EU has promised to do this, and we need to hammer away until we get it!

Good discussion again, gentlemen.

We have one of you seeing the bureaucracy side of the Single Market as a very costly and intrusive system.

The other sees the EU as a pro-active force for the Single Market, and improving the lives of EU citizens.

Can we now move on to FDI and jobs?

Agenda

✓ History & Background
✓ The Nature of the EU
✓ How the EU Works

✓ *Jobs*:
 - The EU Single Market
 - Foreign Direct Investment

Immigration

The Cost of Living

The City & Services

Small Businesses

OK gentlemen, moving on to FDI and jobs.

Let me first clarify things.

Foreign direct investment or FDI is where a company in one country invests directly in another country by establishing operations there itself, or acquiring assets in an existing business of that other country.

It's different from *indirect* investment, which is companies or people investing in the stocks and shares of another country. With FDI, it usually means not only capital investment but management, technology and organisational skills as well.

The big implication is that it means job creation, and the question is, does the UK get FDI because it's in the EU, or are there other reasons? And, if we leave the EU, will that have an impact on FDI and jobs by companies leaving the UK?

So Ken, could you get us started, please.

And remember both of you, what we're looking for is factual data, with a minimum of flim-flam and rhetoric.

Right, multinationals need a base in the EU to gain good access to the Single Market. It's their passport. They invest and are based in the UK for this reason.

They would lose this if the UK moved out of the EU. They'd have to pay EU tariffs and would have more paperwork.

So they would move to an EU member country, taking investment and jobs with them.

We'd end up losing about three million jobs.

Look Ken, based on business surveys, such as that done by Ernst and Young last year, the UK being in the EU is way down the list of reasons for FDI.

Companies invest here because of: (1) the UK's business-friendly culture, (2) it's competitive corporate and personal tax rates, (3) its flexible labour laws, (4) its educated people, (5) its good schools, (6) its political stability, (7) the strength of the economy, (8) the Single Market, and (9) last but not least the English language.

And please stop this stuff about losing three million jobs.
They said the same thing when the UK didn't join the Eurozone.

But some companies have definitely said they would leave the UK if we leave the EU.

Well I'm sorry to have to tell you this Colin, but there are definitely companies saying they'll move out of the UK, taking their investment and jobs with them, if we lose access to the Single Market.

Look Ken, your three million job losses; it has no basis in truth. It's a factoid!

OK Ken, as Mary clarified earlier, you *don't* need to be in the EU to have access to the Single Market! Do these companies know this?

If there are some companies who actually move out we'll have to take the hit, but I doubt they will. It'll cost them in higher taxes.

And what about the millions of lost jobs? You can't just say it's a factoid.

Companies such as Toyota, Nissan, Barclays, HSBC, and Airbus - that's two big car companies, two big banks, and a leading aircraft manufacturer based in Toulouse - are examples of companies who say they'll stay in the UK, whether we remain or leave.

Ken, I'm surprised *you* repeating the three million job losses thing. It's on a Feb. 2016 news sheet by an EU-In campaign group, under the heading *Six Key Facts You Need to Know*. But I wouldn't expect the same thing from you.

The claim goes back to a study done by the National Institute for Economic and Social Research (NIESR), which said:

> *Detailed estimates from input-output tables suggest that up to 3.2 million UK jobs are now associated directly with exports of goods and services to other EU countries. This has given rise to popular concern that some of these jobs might be at risk if Britain were to leave the Union . . . In conjunction with the potential gains from withdrawing . . . there is a case that withdrawal from the EU might actually offer net economic benefits.*

The Director of the NIESR at the time, Dr. Martin Weale, described the 3m job losses claim as "pure Goebbels", referring to Joseph Goebbels, who was Reich Minister for Propaganda in Nazi Germany.

Prof. Iain Begg of the LSE, who authored the 2000 report, said the claim was a "false perspective".

Look Colin, I don't know if you're facing reality here.

Some *governments* have said if we didn't remain in the EU their companies might leave.

The Japanese, for example, with 1,300 firms here and 130,000 jobs, say they'd have to review their position" if we left the EU.

And Ford, which employs about 15,000 in the UK, has made similar comments.

So Ken, why leave?

When we strike a free trade agreement with the EU upon leaving, it will get rid of the protective tariffs.

And don't say we might not be able strike an FTA with the EU. It's to UK/EU mutual advantage.

I suspect, Ken, the worry about not having access to the Single Market may be due to not being aware that you don't need to be in the EU to have access to the EU Single Market.

I think we can move on now guys, but to finish up on FDI, can I say I felt quite saddened hearing about those job losses
in N. Ireland with Bombardier, the Canadian aerospace and transportation Company.

They've been big-time FDI investors in the UK.

But like the steel losses in Port Talbot and other places it's a global thing, and not much to do with the EU. Or is it?

Efficiency and productivity obviously come into it, but it's more than that. So what else do we need to do?

Maybe our next discussion should be on that subject!

Agenda

✓ History & Background
✓ The Nature of the EU
✓ How the EU Works

✓ *Jobs*:
  - The EU Single Market
  - Foreign Direct Investment
  - Repr. by the EU Trade Comm.

  Immigration

  The Cost of Living

Look guys, sorry to spring this on you,
but there's a third angle to the jobs issue.

It concerns *the UK being represented by the
EU Trade Commissioner* in:
(a) the World Trade Organisation (WTO), and
(b) making trade deals around the world for
the EU's 28 member countries as a whole.

So I've added this, OK?

Ken, can you gets us going?

No problem.
This is short and sweet.

The European Union, if counted as one country would be among the top three economies in the world, up there with the USA and China.

So when the EU's Trade Commissioner goes around the world making trade deals with other countries on behalf of the UK and other member countries, it's a big player.

This means it can get better trade deals than the UK, and greater export trade for the UK than the UK could for itself.

More UK export trade means more UK jobs.

I'd agree.
The EU has *bigger* clout.
But the UK could, for itself, do *better*.

But we're largely talking here about deals to cut tariffs.

Tariffs have been coming down globally and getting close to zero now, thanks to the WTO.

So big clout or small, the EU is no longer that important for getting trade deals.

There are also Technical Barriers to Trade or TBTs, which are covered by the WTO and the UN Economic Commission for Europe.

We're well able to represent ourselves with these global bodies. We don't need the EU as a middleman.

Sorry Ken,
but bigger is better

And about your free trade agreement, or FTA, you can't assume that, if we leave the EU, the UK will be able to negotiate favourable terms.

And how long would it take?

Remember the possibility that we'll be *persona non grata*, not welcome in Europe!

If we don't get favourable terms it'll likely meant we'll have to pay import tariffs on important things we import from the EU, making prices higher in the shops.

And things the UK exports to the EU will have to bear EU tariffs, making *UK* products expensive, and losing sales.

But Ken, as I've said, EU import tariffs are now down - to about 1% on average.

And even that doesn't matter, because we're the EU's biggest customer, bigger than the USA.
We import far more *from* EU countries than we export to them. For example, cars from Germany.

It's *their* car prices going up by 8.5% if tariffs are imposed that they need to worry about.

If the UK leaves the EU there *will* be an EU/UK FTA struck fairly quickly, so *EU* jobs are not lost due to *their* exports and jobs being affected.

So you can expect little if any change in that kind of thing after we leave.

Agenda

✓ History & Background
✓ The Nature of the EU
✓ How the EU Works

✓ Jobs:
  - The EU Single Market
  - Foreign Direct Investment
  - Repr. by the EU Trade Comm.

✓ Immigration

The Cost of Living

The City & Services

Small Businesses

OK guys. I've again put a marker on where we are now: *Immigration*.

Or to give it its full title: *Immigration, Open Borders, Free Movement.*

We know immigration has become a big issue.

As a member of the European Union the UK must have open borders and free movement of people with the other 27 member countries.

We allow EU citizens to visit, live, study, work, retire, vote in UK elections, and enjoy all government facilities and all benefits of the United Kingdom, without restriction, just as if they were UK citizens. In fact EU citizenship over-rides UK citizenship. The entitlement is the same for UK citizens in other EU countries.

Then there's the migrant crisis, people fleeing from war in Syria, Iraq, and Afghanistan claiming political asylum, and also economic migrants.

However, this is a related but *separate* issue.

The Dublin Agreement requires migrants to register in the first EU country they enter, but it isn't working, so it may be scrapped, meaning more pressure on the UK to accept migrants.

So who'd like to start us off; Colin?

OK Mary, the big concern with immigration is lack of control over our own borders and about 300,000 people coming in each year

Colin, you've got to accept that open borders is part of the deal in us being a signed-up member of the EU.

And open borders *are* needed if we're to be one *demos*.

But remember, some of these people bring in important skills.

Also, open borders is a two-way street; UK citizens are free to study, work, and settle anywhere in the EU.

It's because of the EU's Fourth Freedom, the movement of *people*, which has a lot to do with trying to make us all one *demos*. It's the real reason for the Fourth Freedom.

But due to high unemployment and poor conditions in Greece, Spain, Croatia, Cyprus, Portugal, Italy, France, Slovakia, Bulgaria, and Romania, hundreds of thousands are flooding into the UK every year. You can't blame them.

And with loose EU border controls in Greece, the situation is worse, with non-EU nationals coming in, including criminals and terrorists.

Your heart goes out to most of these people, but the UK is already the most overcrowded country in the EU. I can't see us taking any more.

I'm not ignoring any of that Colin but, apart from the legal requirement, we have to go with our hearts and do the humanitarian thing.

And Colin, greater population means greater economic activity, greater wealth, greater diversity, and greater strength.

This is the real reason for the Fourth Freedom. It benefits the whole of the EU and each country in it.

Ken, it's no problem for those with needed skills. But we're now very much overcrowded. England is the most overcrowded country in the EU!

As a result:
1. Hospitals are in dire straits, waiting lists are endless, A&E is in tatters, ambulances can't cope.
2. Social Services are exhausted.
3. There are no nursery places.
4. Surgeries are at "breaking point".
5. Schools: no place for your child.
6. An affordable flat/house is almost impossible for the young.
7. They're building homes across our green countryside.
8. Degradation of the environment.
9. Sitting in traffic is normal.
10. Many commuting trains are standing-room only.
11. Wages are pushed right down.
12. We're fighting each other for spaces and places.

And another thing: do you know how many people in the UK speak a European language, while in countries like Germany, the Netherlands, Belgium, and France, almost everyone speaks English?

It's because we're insular, we don't have a European mind-set. We're put at a disadvantage when dealing with people from other European countries.

We don't have good communication with them. No wonder we're looked upon as outsiders.

It's the stereotype of the Englishman who speaks louder to make himself understood.

Ken, you're absolutely right about us not having the European language skills we should have.

But for goodness' sake Ken, you *are* ignoring those effects of the UK being *desperately* overcrowded!

And before you were saying that open borders enable the UK to get the skills it needs.

So how does the USA, Australia, New Zealand, Canada, and most other countries get the skills they need with systems of *controlled* immigration?

Ken, I'm most concerned about your greater population giving us greater wealth, diversity, and strength. It ain't necessarily so.

You may be talking about the *law of comparative economic advantage*: it doesn't need free movement of people.

Look at NAFTA, free trade between Canada, the USA, and Mexico. Free movement of people isn't in it.

Alright Colin, where I'm coming from is separateness versus togetherness.

Free and open borders means understanding and cooperation as one people with our European neighbours.

Maybe I put more weight on this than you do.

And c'mon Colin, you cannot ignore all those boat people, fleeing from war and persecution. We have to do our fair share.

I agree with you, but we don't need to belong to the EU to do our fair share.

I'm not against immigration. What I'm against is *uncontrolled* immigration.

It's fundamental. We need to get back control of our own borders.

Agenda

✓ History & Background
✓ The Nature of the EU
✓ How the EU Works

✓ Jobs:
  - The EU Single Market
  - Foreign Direct Investment
  - Repr. by the EU Trade Comm.

✓ Immigration

  The Cost of Living

  The City & Services

That's probably enough on Immigration. Thank you both for bringing it out as both a heart and a head issue.

Now, who would like to get us started on:
The Cost of Living, and how remaining in or leaving the European Union might have an effect on that?

And let's look at the *whole cost* picture. Ken?

Right, Mary. Looking at the whole cost picture let's start with the EU Budget. We're the second biggest contributor after Germany, but it's only a *fraction* of total UK government spending.

Also: the cost of regulations is much less than the benefits we get back in the Single Market.

Thirdly, something people might complain about is the EU spending on member country infrastructure, such as roads, bridges, and highways.

But if we want Europe to prosper then we have to spend money on these kinds of projects.

Ken, our *net* contribution to the EU Budget is now heading for £20 billion a year.

You can't just dismiss it as a fraction of total govt. spending!

That kind of money would plug a big hole in the NHS budget, help reduce student tuition fees, pay for flood defences, help pay down our mushrooming national debt . . .

. . . you're not seeing the big picture, Colin. We get back a lot more than we give. Just the Single Market alone is worth it all.

I'm seeing the big picture fine! Look at *everybody's* wages pressed down with migrants' low wages.

Pressed-down wages affect the cost of living because a lot of people don't have the *means* of living. At least, not without in-work benefits.

Alright Colin, the migrant effect on wages is due to Eurozone countries not yet being integrated.

If they were, and if all member countries, the UK included, were part of the Eurozone, then that would get the Eurozone going.

So no more migrant effect, and the European Union would be a powerful, global force rivalling the USA.

Sorry Ken, we're not interested in joining the Eurozone.

Even without the UK, the Eurozone will have the same taxation policies, foreign policies, social policies, policing and justice policies, co-ordinated budgets, and funding flowing seamlessly.

It will make the common currency and interest rates work, and put Europe back on full employment and prosperity. It willl resolve the migrant effect, and not just in wages.

Gentlemen, I know I said we should look at the whole cost picture, and it's fine that we've looked at the EU Budget and the impact of the Eurozone.

But we're getting too much into *macroeconomics*, and that's not where we want to go.

We're discussing *The Cost of Living*.

What I'm really interested in is prices in the shops and supermarkets.

Will they increase or decrease if we remain in or leave the European Union?

Colin, why don't you have a go at this.

OK Mary, being a customs union, the EU has *protective import duties* on things coming from outside the EU, such as 11.6% on shoes and clothing and 8.5% on cars. It makes prices higher in the shops and showrooms.

Second, there is the EU Common Agricultural Policy or CAP, intended originally to subsidise French farmers and protect them from cheaper food coming in from outside the EU: It's still making food prices in the shops more expensive.

Third, there is the cost of compliance with EU environmental protection. Of course we want to protect the environment for the sake of our health and other reasons, but we don't really need any lessons from the EU. We could do it more cheaply without all the EU bureaucracy and interference, if we did it ourselves.

It would mean lower gas and electricity bills.

The fourth thing is the cost of EU Single Market bureaucracy. It affects *everybody* and it come out as higher costs across the board for everybody,

Is that all, Colin?

Let's see what Ken has to say . . .

. . . sorry Mary, if you'll permit me, there are a couple of other things.

Fifth, there are rental and housing costs. With such huge numbers of people from the EU coming into the UK, about 300,000 people per year, it pushes up the demand for places to live, and that leads to higher rental and property prices. For example:

With increased property prices *plus* pressed-down wages, it's reported that Londoners now spend on average about *two-thirds* of their pre-tax income on rent, compared to about *half* five years ago.

So the second most basic thing in the household budget after food, namely the cost of a place to live, has gone up a lot because of the EU.

Finally, because VAT is an EU sales tax, as a government we pay a proportion of that to the EU, on top of our EU Budget contribution. If we didn't have to pay that we'd pay less VAT in the shops.

OK Colin, I think that's enough.

I'm sorry Ken, I let Colin go for a bit too long there. But now it's your turn. What do you have for us?

Not a problem, Mary.

Two basic EU benefits have a direct impact on the cost of living, and they are the EU as a Single Market, and the EU as a Customs Union.

First, let's deal with the EU Single Market. It makes prices in the shops cheaper because:

a) its common standards encourage bigger production volumes and greater exports because of EU-wide markets, and lower unit costs as a whole, and

b) it reduces administration, distribution and warehousing costs because it cuts out delays. Delays cost money as they hinder just-in-time supply chains, perishables are subject to spoiling, goods can deteriorate, and the cost of transport increases.

So the EU Single Market is a big factor in reducing costs and making prices cheaper in the shops.

Second, there's the European Union as a Customs Union, where there are no trade tariffs or customs duties between its 28 member countries. It means cheaper prices in the shops.

As for protective traded tariffs imposed on goods coming from countries outside the EU, the EU has arranged bilateral free trade agreements, or FTAs, with about 27 countries around the world. This has cut tariffs and the cost of goods in the shops. The EU Trade Commissioner has been able to cut good deals with countries such as:

Egypt, Iceland, Chile, South Africa, South Korea, Switzerland, Mexico, Turkey, and Norway, plus other smaller countries such as Monaco, the Faroe Islands, and Liechtenstein.

Also, Colin spoke of pressed-down wages, but there's another side to this. If your wage bill is lower you can be more competitive in your pricing, which again means lower prices in the shops.

Agenda

✓ History & Background
✓ The Nature of the EU
✓ How the EU Works

✓ Jobs:
  - The EU Single Market
  - Foreign Direct Investment
  - Repr. by the EU Trade Comm.

✓ Immigration

✓ The Cost of Living

The City & Services

Small Businesses

OK Ken, thanks for that.
I think we now have enough
information on the cost of living.
Good arguments on both sides,
I think.

But now we come to
The City & Services.

The UK financial services sector is a major strength for the UK economy, and for jobs.

It's still known as *The City* but has now spread to other parts of London, especially Canary Wharf, and to other parts of the UK, for example Edinburgh and Glasgow, which are now global centres in their own right.

To be clear, we're talking about banking, both retail and wholesale, insurance, fund management, wealth management, securities dealing, foreign exchange trading, commodities trading, futures trading, accountancy, legal services, management consultancy, and maritime or shipping services.

All this contributes hugely to the UK economy, and the sector gives a very healthy balance of trade.

But there have been disputes between the EU and the UK government over the EU's attempts to control the way the City does business, made worse with the 2008-2009 financial markets crisis, blamed by some on what's seen as unfettered Anglosphere capitalism.

Who'd like to start us off?

OK Mary, I'll start.
A big concern that should make us remain in the EU is its Single Market.

To do business efficiently with Europe we must be *in* Europe. You need a passport, and that passport is being in a country that's in the EU Single Market.

Some big financials, like American firms J.P. Morgan and Goldman Sachs, have hinted they'd leave London if we moved out of the EU, taking their jobs with them.

Some people in the City say we'll die if we leave the EU.

As made clear by Mary, we *don't* need to be in the EU Single Market to have access.

The real concern is the EU's heavy-handed and ham-fisted regulation, which ignores the City's global positioning. It will kill off the City if we stay.

J.P. Morgan and Goldman Sachs are giving mega bucks to the EU-In campaign. Maybe no surprise, since former PM Tony Blair is employed by J.P. Morgan as an advisor.

Mr Blair wanted us to join the Eurozone, saying we'd die if we didn't.

He was stopped by Chancellor Gordon Brown's *Five Tests*, which I think are still relevant today.

Before you do that Colin, let me simply say that we have to stay in to win.

To point out the obvious Colin, this is not about joining the Eurozone. Nobody still wants that, except maybe Mr Blair.

It's not as simple as that, Colin. HSBC is quite a different kind of bank, because it has a lot of its business in Asia.

In comparison, for any bank with a lot of business in Europe, they need to be *in* Europe.

I think they're still relevant, Ken, but let's go back to J.P. Morgan and Goldman Sachs.

You must know of the HSBC announcement. After months of thinking about it they've decided to *stay* in London. Allow me to quote what they're reported as saying.

The UK is an important and globally connected economy. It has an internationally respected regulatory framework and legal system, and immense experience in handling complex international affairs.

London is one of the world's leading international financial centres and home to a large pool of highly skilled, international talent.

It remains, therefore, ideally positioned to be the home base for a global financial institution such as HSBC.

Alright Colin, but my big concern is that if we leave the EU we'll be unable to influence things on behalf of The City.

Chancellor George Osborne has been able to do this a couple of times.

And let me tell you, if the European Commission gets its way in the area of financial services, it will end up a mega-blow for the City. We have to stay in to make sure that doesn't happen.

HSBC? J.P. Morgan? Goldman Sachs? We're talking *global* banks Their concerns are the same.

Look Ken, we have to get out of the EU for City firms to be free of heavy-handed, incessant regulations.

And free from high taxes in the Eurozone, 30% in Germany, 33% in France, versus 20% in the UK.

And the City needs to be free to choose how best to implement accords from the *Basel Committee on Banking Supervision*.

It's the real source of EU banking regulations. The EU itself is a middleman.

Well I can tell you Ken, it's not just the Commission. The French leadership is dead-against anything they see as special treatment for the City.

OK Colin, but you must surely see that, with both Chancellor George Osborne and Prime Minister David Cameron, at least in the area of financial regulations, the UK gets listened to!

We wouldn't even get that from outside the EU!

Alright Ken, I'd have to say that the Chancellor and the Prime Minister appear to have done their best.

And as you say, it'll be a mega-blow if the European Commission were to get its way.

But look, we're just 1 of 28 countries; the French/German coalition controls things; we're out-voted, *every* time.

We don't and wouldn't have the influence you seem to think we would!

If we stay in the City we'll be sucked into more and more EU intervention by an EU mindset that's completely different and doesn't understand the City.

Look Colin, global, uniform rules are essential if we're to avoid a repeat of the banking and financial markets crisis of 2008-2009.

And we've got to stay on side with our European neighbours, and promote the City as a *European* as much as a *UK* asset

We need to convince Europe that, If the City is killed off, business *won't* flow to Paris and Frankfurt but to New York, because only London has built up the critical mass, experience, and network of capabilities to rival it.

Look Ken, if we stay in, the EU will be able to take *any* action they feel is needed to maintain financial stability. This will mean over-regulation. The EU aim is *controlling* financial services, not growth.

In the May, 2015 report, *Where Next Europe: the Future of Financial Services,* it's *over-regulation* about which the City of London Corporation is concerned.

And as you know, the EU leadership is not particularly sympathetic to what they see as unfettered Anglosphere capitalism.

And neither are they happy about *London* as the European, global financial centre.

Well you could hardly blame them for any of that.

Look, the EU carries out its financial services supervision through: *the European Banking Authority,* the *European Securities and Markets Authority*, the *European Insurance and Occupational Pensions Authority*, the *European Systemic Risk Board*, the *Joint Committee of the European Supervisory Authority*, and the respective *national ESAs.*

Sheesh Colin! Do you have to give us all that!

Whoever it is, we'll need to stay on side with them by remaining in the EU, if we want to have influence. Otherwise they'll use some excuse to deny the City access to European markets.

Sorry Ken, you'd be in for a disappointment.

The powers of these different bodies are determined by EU *majority* voting, influenced by the *European Commission.*

These bodies will bring in regulations that suit the *Eurozone, not the City*. Even if we're, in we'll be outsiders.

Right Gentlemen, let me try to sum up, because the issue of the City and the EU is a bit complicated, and that's without getting into the Financial Transactions Tax, which the UK has opted out of but will still affect the City.

On the one hand, Ken, you're saying that we need to remain in the EU so that the City gets the benefit of the EU Single Market.

And we have a better chance to influence the EU in deciding financial regulations that will affect the City. Without this influence, you say, regulations would be against us and the City would die.

Colin, you're saying that it's the heavy hand of EU bureaucracy with its different mind set that will kill off the City. And that, as just one of 28 countries, and with France and Germany in charge, plus the Commission, we have little real influence in the EU.

You say, we're better off implementing ourselves, for example, Basel Committee accords, without the EU as middleman.

Agenda

✓ History & Background
✓ The Nature of the EU
✓ How the EU Works

✓ Jobs:
  - The EU Single Market
  - Foreign Direct Investment
  - Repr. by the EU Trade Comm.

✓ Immigration

✓ The Cost of Living

✓ The City & Services

Small Businesses

Last but not least we come to *Small Businesses*. For some, the EU might be seen as a help. For others, it's a hindrance.

So what can we discuss that might help small businesses decide on EU-In or EU-Out?

But first, let me set the scene.

Napoleon Bonaparte called *us a nation of shopkeepers,* meant to be a slur. But it was taken as a compliment to the UK's entrepreneurial spirit, which small businesses epitomise.

Also, there have been studies showing that the small business sector creates most jobs.

But small business owners need to ask three questions at this time:

1. is the EU good for me and my family,
2. is it good for my business, and
3. is it good for the UK economy and society?

This is where we come in.

Ken, would you like to start us off?

Sure, Mary.

The EU realises the importance of small business. This is why, in 2011, it introduced its Small Business Act, including:

1. the *Think Small First* principle, to reduce regulatory impact and expense on small business

2. the encouragement of family businesses

3. Second chances for small businesses filing for bankruptcy

4. help in getting government contracts

5. legal support in forcing big businesses to pay bills on time

6. easier access to loans and grants.

The problem, Ken, is this:

1. the difference between EU promise versus performance

2. the amount of costly, *time-consuming* EU bureaucracy

3. the nonsensical requirements which have put some *out* of business!

Sole traders, which make up about 75 per cent of small businesses, are usually on the losing side. For them, EU cost is more than EU benefit.

And where's the big cost? It's in *time*. It has been estimated that small businesses spend up to 25% of their time on EU bureaucracy.

I don't know where you got that figure of 3:1, Colin.

But the point is that the EU realises the problems small businesses are having, and it's expected that new EU regs will exclude small businesses from some regulations.

This is the whole point behind the EU's *Think Small First* principle.

And the EU never gives out money they didn't get from us in the first place, except that we get a lot less back it's 3:1.

I got 3:1 by working out how much of our EU Budget contribution goes on a few different areas, then averaging how much we get back.

As for new EU regulations, I can't see the leopard changing its spots.

Promises of EU reform and reduced bureaucracy have been coming and going for a long time.

The EU is simply not capable of changing its bureaucratic, control-everything, regulate-everything mind-set.

That's just an opinion you have Colin, in spite of assurances that the EU is working hard to make things easier for small businesses.

Also, you may be overlooking a big EU benefit for small business.

If a small business has a niche product, the EU Single Market is a great opportunity.

It makes it much easier to reach key markets throughout the EU and its 28 member countries.

And the EU will help you, starting with the EU Small Business Portal.

Hang on Colin, what are you saying here? Is this a criticism of the EU Single Market? What's your point?

I'd agree with you Ken. The EU Single Market can be helpful to small businesses with a niche product or service suitable for export.

But there seems to be an assumption that, because the EU does something helpful, it is *the most* helpful.

Don't you think our own government could better help small business with export opportunities if the EU got out of the way?

For example, we've got the Department of Trade & Industry, Department of Business Innovation & Skills, and International Trade Services for exporters.

If I were a small business owner they would be my first port of call.

Look Colin, we know all about that, so please get down off your soap-box.

The whole idea of the EU Single Market is to make everything conform across the EU so as to make a level playing field, and make things fair and competitive. That's good for small businesses.

On the political and societal, member countries have agreed to share their sovereignty and pool their interests for the collective good.

We give up something to get something better.

My point is that our UK government increasingly gets excluded from *being* a government, for example in promoting small business, because we've a *supra*-government above us in Brussels telling us what to do and how to do it!

Brussels thinks it knows what's best for us, better than we know ourselves!

It's a situation we've got into over the years, with each succeeding treaty.

People may still be thinking that the EU is just free trade.

It *used* to be when it was the EEC, but it's all political and societal control now.

Colin, you can't separate free trade and EU Single Market from the political and societal. They all influence each other.

This is what a *United States of Europe* is about, which is what the EU will become. It's been the aim ever since the 1957 Treaty of Rome.

This is when all countries in the EU will be fully integrated, and this is when the USE will become an economic and political powerhouse to rival the USA!

It'll open up great opportunities for small businesses!

OK, as I've said Ken, I've no problem with a single market and free trade. After all, it was the UK that led the drive for a Single Market.

But EU bureaucracy, for example the Working Time Directive, health and safety regulations, climate change stuff, and regulatory requirements for EU Single Market, are all a big cost and time-hindrance for many small businesses.

Wasn't it *free trade* we signed up for with the EEC in '73?

Sorry Ken, but I can't agree that the best interests of UK small businesses are best understood and handled by a bunch of bureaucrats working in the bureaucracy behemoth in Brussels!

Once again Colin, that's just your opinion, and you're exaggerating.

And again, they make sure that all interested parties are canvassed, so that everyone's interests are represented.

But Colin, be practical! Big business is where most business is!

The Commission has to invite these people to participate fully in developing legislation because they're the ones it will mostly affect!

Ken, The EU *is* such a big and complex behemoth that it takes years, decades, to get anything done.

Second, the big-hitter interested parties are the big business multinationals. They have a reported 30,000 lobbyists in Brussels.

Big business sits on the expert groups and advisory groups the Commission sets up, giving them access to inside information; big biz lobby events are held in the Commission's HQ itself. No wonder big biz loves big EU!

The Corporate Europe Observatory estimates that 80% of the Commission's stakeholders are big biz, and 3% small business.

Allow me to stop you there, Ken and Colin.

This is all interesting stuff, but we're going on too long about big business multinationals as if they were the big, bad bogeyman. It's small business we're interested in.

We need to be moving to a conclusion, so I'd like someone to get us back on track with something a bit more specific and relevant to small businesses.

OK Mary,
something specific.
If we leave the EU it'll mean
painful travel and transport
in Europe, which right now
is easy with no border
controls.

A lot of hauliers and
truckers are small
businesses, and no border
controls gives efficient
logistics. It enables them to
keep costs down, as they
don't have to spend time
being stacked through
Dover or Calais, for
example.

And some of the goods are
to or from small UK
businesses specialising in
perishable foods, which
can easily go off if transport
is delayed.

Look at my trucking through
Europe map.

Ken, I agree travel won't be
as seamless, but let's not
exaggerate the difficulties.
And border controls make it
harder for criminals and
terrorists to get into the UK.

It's the lack of border controls
that has induced the migrant
crisis.

As for hauliers and truckers,
yes, delays and stacking
could be a serious problem.

However, the UK lives or dies
on its exports and imports,
and I've no doubt efficient
border checking with
biometric identification and
other technology will become
normal at Dover and Calais.

OK, let's see your map.

Right Colin, suppose you're bringing a truckload of furniture from Athens, Greece, to Birmingham, or machine parts from Birmingham to Athens: (1) how many border checks would you have to go through? (2) which countries would you go through? (3) Can you see how a borderless EU makes it so much easier?

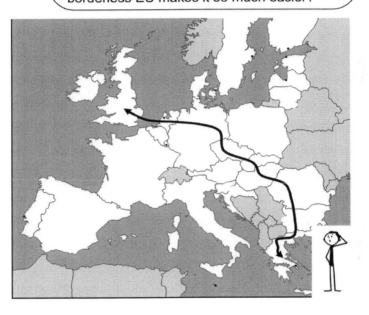

Here's something else: the EU VAT regulations which came into force 01 January, 2015.

You know that VAT is an EU sales tax, and the UK government sends a proportion of VAT collected to the EU.

I agree Colin, it's crazy, and I'm sure the European Commission will do something.

What we need to do is petition our MEPs and European Commission in Brussels as a matter of urgency.

It's obviously against the EU's principle of *Think Small First.*

And I'm sure there are online sole traders who this new regulation affects, so we're agreed on this one.

Well, the EU has re-written the rules, which now forces anyone exporting *digital services* to pay VAT to the EU country in which the *customer* (not the trader) is based.

There's no VAT threshold turnover before you have to register, so it's hitting some online sole traders badly.

It means that if you have customers in ten EU countries then you have to go through ten different VAT tax and admin. processes to stay on-side with EU law.

Agenda

✓ History & Background
✓ The Nature of the EU
✓ How the EU Works

✓ Jobs:
  - The EU Single Market
  - Foreign Direct Investment
  - Repr. by the EU Trade Comm.

✓ Immigration

✓ The Cost of Living

✓ The City & Services

✓ Small Businesses

OK guys, I think that's a good way of ending our discussion. You've done brilliantly!

I'm ready to go, and we all deserve a good lunch at the Rose & Crown.

But I should ask "Is there any other business?" No?

OK then, let's have a summing up. Ken, you've got the floor, then Colin.

Thanks Mary, so let me summarise.

The European Union and our being in it is about peace, understanding, and bringing an end to war. And being one *demos*, one people, one family.

It's about prosperity, strength, efficiency, and being competitive. And it is about quality of life and equality itself for working men and women. All this with freedom of movement of goods, services, capital, and people.

As the EU moves to being a United States of Europe it still isn't perfect. It's a work in progress.

So if the United Kingdom remains in the European family we can influence it for the good. Indeed, it would be a disaster for the UK and the EU if we were to leave.

The EU and ever-closer union is about bigger markets, greater efficiencies of scale, legislative uniformity, freedom of movement, flexibility in channelling resources to where needed, protection against bank failure, and greater prosperity overall.

We *must* vote to remain in Europe!

Thank you Mary, and Ken.

If we remain in the EU, it will mean, firstly societal failure with mass immigration, secondly economic failure and risk, due to worsening of the Eurozone, and thirdly democratic failure with the increasing power of the EU over our daily lives.

If we leave we'll have broken out of a very costly, supra-governmental bureaucracy in Brussels, controlled by unelected bureaucrats who believe they know what's best for us, over-riding our laws.

We'll also be able to control our own borders.

We stayed out of the Eurozone in spite of some people saying we'd be ruined, with millions of jobs at risk. They're saying the same about us leaving the EU.

As for EU reform, it just isn't going to happen.

This island nation – a dynamic combination made up of Scotland, Wales, Northern Ireland and England - has the fifth biggest economy in the world, an international tradition and outlook, and *so* many strengths.

We'll have access to the Single Market, and be free to forge our own, better future in a bigger world.

EU REFORMS: WHAT THE GOVERNMENT GOT

Now let's look at the Prime Minister's efforts between November 2015 and February 2016 to achieve EU reforms.

What were the reform aims and proposals, what was agreed, and what difference did it all make?

Background

In January, 2013, Prime Minister David Cameron made a speech at the London HQ of <u>Bloomberg</u>, when he laid out his EU reform *aims*:

- *Power flowing back to Member States.*

- *A leaner, less bureaucratic ["more competitive"] union.*

- *Movement away from a European Court of Justice which has consistently supported greater centralisation*

- *Fundamental, far-reaching change.*

- *Big, institutional changes*

In October-November 2015 the PM visited EU leaders to discuss these aims and, on 10 November, made a speech at <u>Chatham House</u> in which he laid out his EU reform *proposals*, putting them in a letter to Donald Tusk, European Council President.

EU reforms:
What the government got

P.M. David Cameron

**Donald Tusk
European
Council
President**

10 DOWNING STREET
LONDON SW1A 2AA

THE PRIME MINISTER   10 November 2015

Dear Donald,

**A NEW SETTLEMENT FOR THE UNITED KINGDOM IN A
REFORMED EUROPEAN UNION**

Thank you for inviting me to write setting out the areas where I am seeking
reforms to address the concerns of the British people over our membership of
the European Union.

**Jean-Claude Juncker.
European Commission President.
Key member in the process.**

Mr Cameron then had meetings with Mr Tusk which resulted in a draft agreement, at the conclusion of which the PM announced success.

The draft proposals were put to a summit meeting of EU leaders on 18-19 February, at which the proposals were mostly agreed.

What they said after the summit meeting:

David Cameron, UK Prime Minister

"The UK got special status… we're not bound to ever-closer union… we have protection for the pound… Britain will never be part of a European super state."

George Osborne, UK Chancellor
"We have achieved substantial, fundamental change."

Angela Merkel, German Chancellor
"I don't think we gave the UK too much."

Francois Hollande, French President

"No revision of treaties is planned"

Daila Grybauskaite, Lithuanian President

"Everyone will have their own drama, then we will agree."

In the following pages we will look at the reform *aims* (as described in the Bloomberg speech), the *proposals* (as described in the Chatham House speech), and what was actually *agreed* at the EU summit meeting.

IMMIGRATION

Aim:
Giving more power back to Member States in controlling immigration.

Proposal:
When there are exceptional levels of migration, migrants from EU member countries must live in the UK for four years before claiming benefits

Agreed: in-work benefits
"The Council would authorise Member States to limit the access of newly arriving EU workers to non-contributory in-work benefits for a total period of up to four years from the commencement of employment."

"The limitation should be graduated, from an initial complete exclusion but gradually increasing access to such benefits to take account of the growing connection of the worker with the labour market of the Member State."

"The authorisation would have a limited duration and apply to EU workers newly arriving during a period of 7 years."

Agreed: child benefits
"A proposal to amend Regulation (EC) No. 883/2004 of the European Parliament and of the Council on the coordination of social security systems in order to give Member States, with regard to the exportation of child benefits to a Member State other than that where the worker resides, an option to index such benefits to the conditions of the member state where the child resides."

"This should apply only to new claims made by EU workers in the host Member State. However, as from 1 January 2020, all member states may apply indexation to existing claims to child benefits already exported by EU workers."

"The Commission does not intend to propose that the future system of optional indexation of child benefits be extended to other types of exportable benefits, such as old-age pensions."

Social housing benefits
No agreement was sought on changes in entitlement to social housing benefits.

Comment
The curtailment of in in-work benefits was referred to as an "emergency brake" on benefits provided there was agreed to be *exceptional levels of migration.*

There was little change on child benefits.

The Migration Observatory at Oxford University said that cutting migrant benefits would have "small" impact on immigration, since migrants come not for benefits but higher UK wages, which (e.g.) are six time higher than in Romania.

With the Living Wage coming in, this increases the UK minimum hourly pay rate, so that benefits will have less importance for migrants.

SELF-GOVERNMENT (SOVEREIGNTY)

Aim
"Power flowing back to Member States"

Proposal
"The role of national parliaments should be enhanced by groups of parliaments acting together to stop unwanted EU legislation. This would allow 55% of member country national parliaments to club together to block EU measures"

(the so-called 'red card')

Proposal
"The EU commitment to subsidiarity should be fully implemented."

Agreed
"The member states should discontinue the consideration of a draft legislative act where a number of national parliaments object to it on the grounds of subsidiarity, unless the concerns raised can be accommodated."

The final summit meeting agreement appears to have changed from that given by Mr Tusk.

It responds to *two* proposals, for (a) the red card, and (b) the subsidiarity principle. It still appears to limit the time, for getting 55% of member states together, to 12 weeks - for the objection to be placed on the Council agenda.

4. Comment
If the UK can get (1) 55% support from among the 27 other Member States, (2) the interpretation of "subsidiarity" and whether it applies in a particular case is agreed, and (3) the time limit of 12 weeks to coordinate a response among member states can be met - then the item will be included on the Council's agenda.

SELF-GOVERNMENT (SOVEREIGNTY)

Aim
"Power flowing back to Member States"

Proposal
"Britain should <u>not</u> have an obligation to work toward ever-closer union."

Agreed
"The proposed Decision of the Heads sets out principles to ensure mutual respect between Member States taking part in further deepening of the Economic and Monetary Union and those which do not."

"By doing that we can pave the way for further integration within the Euro area while safeguarding the rights and competences of non-participating Member States."

"The respect for these principles . . . cannot constitute a veto nor delay urgent decisions."

4. Comment
Progression to ever-closer union is a principle in the 1957 Treaty of Rome and in each treaty since then, is promoted by the European Commission and by Eurozone leaders, and is actively supported by the European Court of Justice.

There may be a problem with this agreement holding firm, and with the ECJ picking it apart.

LESS BUREAUCRACY

Aim
A leaner, less bureaucratic union (now referred to as "greater competitiveness")

Proposal
"The UK would like to see a target to cut the total regulatory burden on business."

Agreed
"The EU must increase efforts towards enhancing competitiveness, along the lines set out in the Declaration of the European Council on competitiveness. To this end the relevant EU institutions and the member states will make all efforts to strengthen the internal market . . . this means lowering administrative burdens."

Comment
The EU has been aiming to cut the regulatory burden and EU bureaucracy since the Laeken Declaration of 2001, and the newly appointed First VP Frans Timmermans can issue a veto if a regulation is considered excessive.

There is also an annual audit of EU regulation which has the aim of reducing red tape.

This is not a new or controversial issue. However, there may be some questions as to whether the history, culture and mindset of the EU will allow any real change.

MOVEMENT AWAY FROM THE EUROPEAN COURT OF JUSTICE

Aim
"Movement away from a European Court of Justice that has consistently supported greater centralisation"

2. Proposal
This aim did not convert into a proposal, but it was reported in the media that UK MPs have been pushing for primacy restored in legislation and in legal judgements and opinions, as against the European Court of Justice (ECJ).

In other words the ECJ should not, in future, be able to over-ride UK institutions.

It was also reported that the Prime Minister dropped hints about a new, constitutional court and/or constitution to be created, to defend the UK's Parliament and courts from being over-ridden by EU legislation and the ECJ.

But the UK's senior judge, Lord Neuberger, commented that this would be unworkable. Germany has tried a similar thing with constitutional court to review EU laws, but with little effect.

Nothing announced by the Prime Minister
The aim did not convert into a proposal.

The ECJ and its primacy in over-riding national parliaments and national courts is embedded in EU treaties and in the *Acquis Communautaire*, the EU body of law. These are EU *acquired powers*, not to be returned to member states.

PROTECTING THE CITY AND THE POUND

Aim
Protection of the City and the Pound Sterling.

This aim was added at the summit meeting.

Proposal
"That the Euro is not the only currency of the European Union, to ensure countries outside the Eurozone are not materially disadvantaged . . . and that non-Eurozone members will not have to contribute to Eurozone bailouts."

Agreed
"The single rulebook is to be applied by all credit institutions and other financial institutions to ensure the level playing field within the internal market."

There was also an agreement preventing the European Central Bank forcing payments in Euros to be cleared in a Eurozone member state.

And an agreement that there should be an emergency safeguard to prevent firms being forced to re-locate from the City into the Eurozone.

4. Comment
These agreements were added at the EU summit, and may be incomplete as given above.

At the summit meeting France was reported as being particularly adamant in not wanting the UK to be given any exceptions to the rules of the EU, especially in relation to the City, which was the reason for mention of a "level playing field".

The agreements do not prevent the City being subjected to further EU strictures on the way it does its business, or being compelled to follow the dictates of the majority Eurozone members.

Why the EU reform proposals
could not involve any real change

The basic reason why the EU reform proposals could not involve any real change is to be found in the EU principle of *engrénage.*

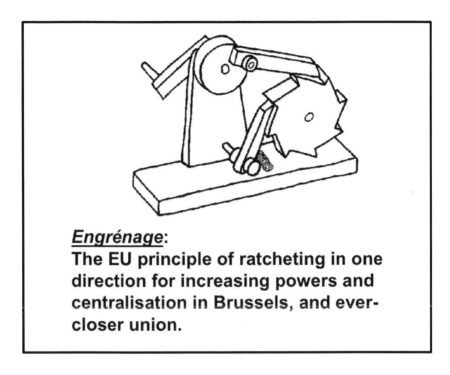

<u>Engrénage</u>:
The EU principle of ratcheting in one direction for increasing powers and centralisation in Brussels, and ever-closer union.

There is no precedent for powers being returned by the EU to national governments, and it is very unlikely that it ever would be.

As French President Francois Hollande said at the summit meeting:

"No revision of treaties is planned."

It is always ever-closer union, never less, in every treaty.

This can be seen as either a good thing or a bad thing but, as far as the Prime Minister's hoped-for reforms are concerned, the EU engrénage principle almost certainly means that they have made no real difference.

EU Reforms: Were they got or not? Circle YES or NO

The PM's Chatham House speech
- Power flowing back to Member States   ...   YES / NO
- A leaner, less bureaucratic union   ....   YES / NO
- Movement away from a European   ....   YES / NO
  Court of Justice that has consistently.........   YES / NO
  supported greater centralisation   ....   YES / NO
- Fundamental, far-reaching change   ....   YES / NO
- Big institutional changes   ....   YES / NO

In which most UK citizens most interested
- Enabling/allowing significant reduction
  in the level of immigration   ....   YES / NO

Announced after meetings with Mr Tusk
- An end to something for nothing
  welfare for EU migrants   ....   YES / NO
- A 'red card' system for
  national parliaments to block
  unwanted EU laws ....   YES / NO
- No more British taxpayers' money
  being used to bail out the Eurozone   ....   YES / NO
- An agreement that we keep the Pound,
  never join the Euro, and fair treatment
  for our currency   ....   YES / NO
- No more British taxpayers' money
  being used to bail out the Eurozone   ....   YES / NO
- Britain out of 'ever-closer union'
  so we do not become part of a
  European Super state   ....   YES / NO

For many of us there is just one, basic question in deciding how to vote on the forthcoming UK Referendum to remain in or leave the European Union:

Are we better off in or out?

The next section offers a way of answering the question, and making it easier for you to decide.

Better off In or Out?
You decide

Soft/Indirect benefits of *Remaining*	Soft/Indirect benefits of *Leaving*
Hard/Direct benefits of *Remaining*	Hard/Direct benefits of *Leaving*

There have been a number of attempts to compare and quantify the costs vs benefits of remaining in or leaving the EU, and the impact on jobs and the economy.

But there are problems:

- The great difficulty in getting reliable numbers for hard/direct costs and benefits.
- The impossibility of putting numbers on the soft/indirect costs and benefits.
- Political agenda, vested interests, bias, and assumptions having the effect of distorting the numbers.
- And so the difficulty in making any cost vs benefit, jobs, or economic estimates reliable and believable.

So an alternative approach is to identify what are said to be the hard/soft benefits of remaining vs leaving - with little or no numbers.

And then to put our own weighting or score on each one.

This way we avoid the above problems by simply getting a big-picture comparison.

It's a rough way of looking at the question but it should provide good-enough information for:

Are we better off in or out?

The different benefits are shown in four tables:

- A. Benefits of remaining: *soft/indirect*
- B. Benefits of remaining: *hard/direct*
- C. Benefits of leaving: *soft/indirect*
- D. Benefits of leaving: *hard/direct*

Each stated benefit is accompanied by an *Alternative View.*

The column on the right is for inserting your own weighting score (from zero to ten).

If you fully agree with a stated benefit and feel it's very important, then you might give it a ten. Or, if you fully agree with the *Alternative View*, then you might give the stated benefit a zero.

At the end of each table there is space for putting *Other Benefits*, if you have them.

If you have read the discussion between Mary, Ken, and Colin in the previous section, this should help in making the assessments.

And of course, if you're been able to get useful information from other sources then that could be factored in as well.

You might want to read through all four tables first, and then come back to give your scores.

Comparison of total scores might then help you to decide on EU In or Out according to your own values and priorities.

A. Benefits of remaining: *soft/indirect*

1. Peace, understanding, security	
2. Being part of the European *demos*	
3. Avoiding Scotland leaving the UK	
4. Remaining at the top table	
5. Freedom of movement	
6. Protecting workers' rights	
7. Protecting the environment	
8. Avoiding isolation	
9. Promoting democracy	
10. Avoiding the unknown	
Total Score	

B. Benefits of remaining: *hard/direct*

1. Avoidance of three million jobs lost	
2. Being part of the EU Single Market	
3. Zero EU tariffs	
4. Represented by EU with bigger clout	
5. Attracting Foreign Direct Investment (FDI)	
6. Payouts to British farmers	
7. Structural funding to regional areas	
8. Positive economic impact of migrants	
9. Climate targets and energy integration	
10. Protective capital by banks	
11. Safeguards for cross-border payments	
12. Avoidance of leaving costs	
Total Score	

C. Benefits of leaving: *soft/indirect*

1. Regained control over our borders	
2. Regained primacy of our laws	
3. Regained primacy of our courts	
4. Regained sovereignty in the regions	
5. Ending erosion of national identity	
6. Regained control over our JHA	
7. Restored relationships with the world	
8. Regained control over vital interests	
9. The restoration of democracy	
10. Ending societal breakdown	
Total Score	

D. Benefits of leaving: *hard/direct*

1. No more contributions to the EU Budget	
2. No more demands for Budget top-ups	
3. Protective tariffs gone: lower shop prices	
4. Reduced VAT: lower shop prices	
5. Cutting the costs of the EU single market	
6. Banished CAP: lower food prices	
7. Banished CFP: regained fishing wealth	
8. Ending costs of Working Time Directive	
9. Regained rights to make FTAs	
10. Not being dragged down by the Eurozone	
11. Property/rental price rises: contained	
12. In-work and child benefits: down	
Total Score	

A. Benefits of remaining: *soft/indirect*

1. Peace, understanding, security The European Union promotes peace and understanding, makes us safer and more secure, and helps avoid war. There's safety (and shared interests) in numbers. **Alternative view:** The threat to European peace has been from Soviet/Russian expansionism. Against this it has not been the EU but NATO which has proven effective in preserving peace.	
2. Being part of the European *demos* By remaining in the EU we remain part of the European *demos*, people, and family. **Alternative view:** A European *demos* is an idealistic and unhelpful myth. We clearly have good relations with our Continental Europe neighbours, but forcing us to be one demos – by insisting on the free movement of people and open borders – is not the way.	
3. Avoiding Scotland leaving the UK If Scotland wishes to remain in the EU and the UK also votes to remain, the risk of Scotland wanting to separate and be totally independent of the UK is avoided. **Alternative view:** If Scotland were to remain in the EU it would increasingly lose its freedom and independence to a government centralised in Brussels; no devolution. Scottish identity would fade. Realising this, the people of Scotland are most likely to prefer devolved government as part of the UK.	

A. Benefits of remaining: *soft/indirect*

---

4. Remaining at the top table
By remaining a member we remain at the EU top table and at the heart of Europe.

If we remain in the EU we can influence it in the right direction and for UK interests.

Alternative view: The real *global* top tables are: the World Trade Organisation (WTO), on which the UK could regain its seat if it left the EU; the United Nations, on which the UK is a member of the Security Council; G2O, of which the UK is a leading member nation.

The French-German coalition controls the EU, with Belgium, Luxembourg, the Netherlands, and Italy: the original six. This is the EU top table and the heart of the EU.

Then there is the Eurozone, which is the next inner circle, of which the UK is not a part either. The UK is on the outer, third circle of non-Eurozone countries.

Finally, the UK has very little real influence, as one of 28 EU member countries. We're *always* out-voted. The numbers, the history, and the experience tell us that we are *not* at the heart or at the top table of the EU.

A. Benefits of remaining: *soft/indirect*

<table>
<tr><td>

5. Freedom of movement

UK citizens can move freely and live, work, study, or retire anywhere in an EU of open borders, which they could not do if the UK were not part of the EU.

Alternative view: It's true that freedom of movement will not be as simple if the UK leaves the EU. For example, if you're going on holiday to an EU country you will need to show your UK (biometric) passport, and at peak times there will be delays.

And you will not be able to say: "I think I'll go look for a job in Poland tomorrow".

As for studying in the EU: little if any change. The same with retirement in an EU country.

The difference would be border controls restored and immigration controlled.

Upon leaving the EU it would be *quid pro quo*, with the UK and EU exchanging freedom of movement rights.

It would be against EU interests to have anything different.

</td><td></td></tr>
</table>

A. Benefits of remaining: *soft/indirect*

<table>
<tr><td>

6. Protecting workers' rights
There is better protection of workers' rights within the European Union against greedy bosses who give themselves excessive salaries, bonuses and stock options but pay and treat ordinary employees poorly.

Alternative view: This may be the official trade union view, and it has truth to it.

The global markets crisis of 2008/2009 is generally recognised to have been partly due to the down-side of unfettered capitalism.

Also, just as wages have been pressed down with large-scale immigration, they will rise if this is halted or slowed down with restored control of borders.

The Labour movement was originally against the EEC as the EU then was, starting with Clement Atlee himself. But everything changed when Jacques Delors addressed the TUC Congress in 1998 and turned Labour in the other direction.

There must be not so much protection, of workers' rights but, more positively, recognition of mutual interests between management and employees. There are ways of achieving this, with Scandinavian countries and some UK companies leading the way.

But also this should not and must not be done by a level of supra-government above UK government. We would be much better off doing this for ourselves.

</td><td>

</td></tr>
</table>

A. Benefits of remaining: *soft/indirect*

7. Protecting the environment There is better protection of the environment within the EU. Climate change and carbon emissions, for example, have been tackled by the EU, and to guarantee this continuing we must remain in the EU. **Alternative view:** The UK has now established respectable credentials showing that we are at least as green as other EU countries, with the possible exception of Germany. But things have gone too far, so that the benefit now outweighs the cost. For example costly solar energy and poor flood control measures. We do not need to be part of the EU to protect the environment, we can well do this far better for ourselves. We do not need a level of supra-government above us to do it for us, forcing us into doing things which do not make sense.	

A. Benefits of remaining: *soft/indirect*

8. Avoiding isolation By remaining in the EU the UK avoids being cut off from the world, alone, isolated, and its reputation in the world diminished. **Alternative view:** It's quite the opposite. For several reasons the UK would recover and take back its place in the world, for example getting back its seat on the WTO. We have always been *internationalist*, and the UK is a member of about 100 international organisations, has a seat on the UN Security Council, charities such as Oxfam have a global outreach, we're a leading member country of G20, and of course we're in the Commonwealth.	

A. Benefits of remaining: *soft/indirect*

9. Promoting Democracy The EU is a European and global force for promoting democracy, and the UK is a vital part of this. The UK is the mother of all parliaments, and the long history of hard-won democratic values in the UK is an example and inspiration to the rest of the EU. The EU was there for Eastern bloc nations as a bastion of democracy when they became free of Soviet domination. Any country which wishes to join the EU must first show or develop democratic institutions. The European External Action Service goes around the world promoting peace, defending human rights, providing humanitarian aid, and democratic values. So we must remain in the EU to support the EU in its mission of promoting democracy and democratic values. **Alternative view:** All of this sounds fine, but the problem is that the EU is redundant. There are any number of international, government, NGO, and charitable organisations that do the same and similar things.	

A. Benefits of remaining: *soft/indirect*

10. Avoiding the unknown Remaining in the EU means staying as we are, with the status quo but, because it still isn't perfect, working for EU reform. It avoids taking a jump into the void and avoiding a big, unnecessary risk. **Alternative view:** There is no status quo if we remain in the EU; it would be ever-increasing control by Brussels – in spite of any promises that the UK would not have to join the Eurozone. UK exit plans are ready, albeit not officially. For example, there would be a UK/EU free trade agreement, as there already are between the EU and 27 other countries.	

Other *soft/indirect* benefits of remaining?
Put them and score them here

B. Benefits of remaining: *hard/direct*

---

1. Avoidance of three million jobs lost
Based on figures available from the Office of National Statistics (ONS) and the House of Commons Library (HCL), leaving the EU would mean at least three million jobs lost for the UK if we left the European Union.

That's how much trade we do in exports to the EU, which would be lost if UK exporters had to pay EU external tariffs, and did not have full access to the EU Single Market.

Alternative view: The same argument and claim was made when it was said we would lose three million jobs if we didn't join the Euro.

Quoting the ONS and the HCL as sources on important topics like this is deceptive; the generally accepted way of quoting sources is to quote them specifically, so they can be checked up on.

The claim is based on a 2000 report by Prof. Iain Begg for the National Institute of Economic and Social Research (NIESR). Dr Martin Weale, director of the NIESR, referred to the claim of three million job losses as "pure Goebbels".

It's very unlikely that there would be UK job losses, since the UK is the biggest export market for the EU, and EU exporters to the UK would not want any changes that might risk their own exports and jobs. A UK/EU free trade agreement (FTA) would be made: no job losses on either side.

B. Benefits of remaining: *hard/direct*

---

2. Being part of the EU Single Market
The EU Single Market means uniform regulations and standards for goods and services in all 28 member countries. Being part of this market, gives UK producers and distributors easy and efficient access, with greater exports and jobs.

Alternative view: A Single Market is clearly of benefit. However, as a member of the EU the <u>net</u> benefit to the UK is likely *nil or negative* because, as a member, EU bureaucracy *applies across the entire UK economy*.

For the Single Market we have three options:

- Remaining in the EU Single Market as is.

- Leaving the EU and *still* having access to the Single Market through an *FTA*, resulting in:
  - no EU import tariffs
  - lower import costs from *outside* the EU
  - possibly being consulted on standards

- Leaving the EU and *still* having access but *not* having an FTA, resulting in:
  - facing EU tariffs, yet…
  - lower import costs from outside the EU, although…
  - not being consulted on standards.

To make things clear, the UK does <u>not</u> need to be in the EU to have access to the Single Market. But it <u>does</u> have to bear the burden and cost of Single Market bureaucracy across the whole economy so long as it remains a member.

Not being consulted isn't really a problem as standards and regulations often come from global bodies. The EU is a middleman.

B. Benefits of remaining: *hard/direct*

3. Zero EU tariffs Being part of the EU customs union means there are no trade tariffs on exports or imports to/from the *EU* market. This means cheaper prices both ways, and more exports to the EU so more UK jobs. **Alternative view:** Thanks to the work of the WTO trade tariffs are now close to zero. The benefit, even though small, is disappearing.	
4. Represented by the EU with bigger clout Being represented by the EU Trade Commissioner on *global* markets means the UK is given stronger representation. This means better trade deals than if the UK were to represent itself, which means more UK exports and more jobs. **Alternative view:** The EU Trade Commissioner negotiates reduced tariffs/duties which globally, as above, are approaching zero, and what is known as *Technical Barriers to Trade* (TBTs). The EU often acts as middleman on TBTs, for such organisations as the WTO, the *UN Economic Commission for Europe* (UNECE), and the *International Standards Organisation* (ISO). There are about 50 global standard-setting organisations. The EU middleman isn't needed.	

B. Benefits of remaining: *hard/direct*

5. Attracting foreign direct investment (FDI) Being in the EU and its Single Market attracts foreign companies to invest directly in the UK, meaning more UK jobs. **Alternative view:** Surveys show that most companies invest in the UK mostly for its business-friendly culture, low taxes, and other reasons, not because it's in the EU or its Single Market.	
6. Payouts to British farmers British farmers receive payouts from the EU, which stabilises and protects farmers' livelihoods and food production. **Alternative view:** The money comes originally from the UK (in its contribution to the EU Budget), part of which comes back in payouts to farmers. More money would be available to farmers without the EU as middleman. And farmers could well do without the EU paperwork.	

B. Benefits of remaining: *hard/direct*

7. Structural funding to regional areas The EU provides payouts for structural projects in certain areas of the UK to create jobs and opportunities in these areas. **Alternative view:** The money comes originally from the UK, part of which comes back in payouts to regional areas. More money would be available without the EU as middleman.	
8. Positive economic impact of migrants The UK benefits economically from the skills and hard work of immigrants, and a bigger population due to immigration **Alternative view:** The UK does not need to be in the EU to attract migrants with needed skills. A bigger population does not necessarily mean greater wealth.	
9. Climate targets and energy integration EU climate targets focus on emissions cuts, renewables, bioenergy, and energy efficiency/savings. Energy integration is aimed at integrated policies across the EU. **Alternative view:** EU climate targets are made complex and more expensive with EU integrated energy policies. Germany as the leading country has seen big increases in green levies and the cost of energy, and overlapping and inflexible EU regulation is adding to costs.	

B. Benefits of remaining: *hard/direct*

10. Protective capital held by banks Following the 2008/2009 global markets crisis this EU regulation imposes the proportion of equity required to ensure banks are prudently managed, so reducing the risk of taxpayer-funded government bail-outs. **Alternative view:** The regulation comes largely from the *G20* group and the *Basel Committee,* in which the Bank of England plays a key role. The EU is more or less a middleman.	
11. Safety rules for cross-border payments The aim of the rules is to combat fraud in internet payments, improve efficiency, and cut costs in EU cross-border payments. **Alternative view:** These are good rules, but it's another example of EU redundancy. Safety in cross-border payments is a global need; it does not require the EU as a middleman.	

B. Benefits of remaining: *hard/direct*

12. Avoidance of leaving costs If the UK leaves the EU there will be big costs in leaving, which of course would be avoided if we remain. The costs of negotiating exit, negotiating new trade agreements with other countries, changes in laws and regulations, changes in processes, and other unforeseeable costs would all be avoided if we remain. **Alternative view:** The costs would not be so much costs but an *investment* - for much greater gain.	

Other *hard/direct* benefits of remaining?
Put them and score them here

C. Benefits of leaving: *soft/indirect*

1. Regained control over our borders As long as the UK is a member of the European Union, the UK has little control over its own *borders*, or over immigration from the other 27 EU member countries, or the seven countries (including Turkey) waiting to join. **Alternative view:** The UK government does aim to control immigration by restricting benefits, and the trends that became clear in 2015 may force the EU to bring in more practical policies to control immigration.	
2. Regained primacy of our laws As long as the UK is a member of the EU, the laws (and courts) of the UK Parliament, Scottish Parliament, Welsh Assembly, and N. Ireland Stormont, are over-ridden by *EU* laws (and courts), which now, directly or indirectly, accounts for most UK legislation. **Alternative view:** It is arguable as to how much UK legislation the EU actually accounts for, and the UK Parliament is always given the opportunity to scrutinise EU legislation. UK governments freely signed up to the treaties behind these laws. They are no different from other international laws.	

C. Benefits of leaving: *soft/indirect*

3. Regained primacy of our courts As long as the UK is a member of the EU, Scottish, Welsh, English and N. Ireland courts are over-ridden by the European Court of Justice (ECJ). There are no appeals. The ECJ mission is to support the European Commission and commitment to ever-closer political union. It has both a judicial and a *political* role. It is not a neutral court Whenever the UK has brought a case to the ECJ it has always lost. **Alternative view:** Without the ECJ the EU wouldn't work. It makes sure that EU rules and regulations are applied and enforced in the same way throughout the EU, not just for the UK but for all EU member countries. The ECJ also prevents any member country from causing a breakdown in EU law and the EU as whole not working.	

C. Benefits of leaving: *soft/indirect*

4. Regained Sovereignty in the regions Structural EU funding to *notional* regions of Scotland, Wales, England, and N. Ireland comes under direct control of the EU *Committee of the Regions*. For every £3 billion we give through the EU budget we get about £1 billion back, much of which is spent on white elephant projects. Direct relationships are promoted between Brussels and these notional regions (e.g. parts of Scotland, West Wales, Cornwall). This accords with the EU interpretation of *subsidiarity*, where the EU has the aim of by-passing *national* governments. Leaving the EU would end this EU intrusion between national and regional. **Alternative view:** EU subsidiarity gives greater power to regions, which is good for regional self-government, and it provides funds that they might not otherwise get. But this is something on which the EU might consider reform, as it wouldn't go against any fundamental EU principles such as the free movement of goods, services, capital, and people.	

C. Benefits of leaving: *soft/indirect*

<table>
<tr><td>

5. Ending erosion of national identity
UK citizenship is over-ridden by EU citizenship. For example, passports and driving licenses are EU.

The European Union is legally a real country, with flag, anthem, national day, and virtually the full array of executive, legislative, and judicial resources, aiming to become and be known as the United States of Europe (USE), with one *demos*.

Loyalty to the EU is promoted with publicity and educational material in schools, even at infants level, with the aim of displacing national identities.

Leaving would put a stop to the attempted displacement and erosion of Scottish, Welsh, N. Ireland, English, and UK identities.

Alternative view: A member country agrees by treaty to share its sovereignty and identity in the collective body of the European Union.

It is not an erosion of national identity but a pooling of sovereignty for the good of each country, and the good of all.

We may give up a little, but we get a lot back.

</td><td></td></tr>
</table>

C. Benefits of leaving: *soft/indirect*

6. Regained control over our JHA A lot of policies on Justice and Home Affairs (JHA) are controlled by the EU. Leaving the EU we would regain full control over our JHA. *Interpol*, for example, enables police forces around the world, not just Europe, to cooperate in catching criminals and terrorists. International cooperation and data sharing on criminal activity and terrorism does not require the EU. It's redundant. And the *European Arrest Warrant* allows a UK citizen to be falsely or unjustly arrested and transported without UK authorities having any say, because we do not have control over our own JHA. **Alternative view:** In a world where criminals and terrorists can communicate and move effortlessly across national boundaries, JHA is much more effective in combating them when it's the same and borderless throughout the EU.	

C. Benefits of leaving: *soft/indirect*

7. Restored relationships with the world
The European External Action Service (EEAS), with offices in 140 countries, aims to displace member country representation, presence and relationships around the world.

It tells our foreign relations people and diplomats what to say and do in areas where the EU has taken over powers or *competences* to act.

Leaving the EU would fully restore UK representation, presence and relationships around the world.

Alternative view: The EEAS doesn't displace UK diplomatic presence. As a major power it represents EU member countries as a whole more effectively and efficiently and, because of its bigger presence, it gets listened to.

It has greater clout.

The EEAS is a force for good around the world.

C. Benefits of leaving: *soft/indirect*

8. Regained control over vital interests As one of 28 member states the UK has no veto and little power to protect its vital interests against the majority in the European Parliament or European Council. It is not part of the 'inner six' circle, or a member of the Eurozone, and it is always out-voted. It has never succeeded in any case brought to the European Court of Justice. By leaving the EU the UK would regain control over its vital interests. **Alternative view:** If member countries were given veto power to protect so-called vital interests, then EU progress would be stymied. Things wouldn't and couldn't get done. Majority vote is the only way, and there is nothing to stop the UK from arguing its case. Collectively, the EU as a whole makes better decisions for the EU as a whole.	

C. Benefits of leaving: *soft/indirect*

9. The restoration of democracy UK democracy would be restored by leaving the EU. The EU has a different meaning for *democracy*, compared with the meaning understood by most people in the UK. It is democracy handed down by "wise guardians" (based on Plato's *Republic*), in other words the *European Commission* and its President, who are said to see themselves as these wise guardians The EU Parliament, with (a) each UK Brussels-based MEP trying to represent nearly one million UK citizens, (b) little genuine, open debate in the EU Parliament, on (c) legislation initiated exclusively by an unelected European Commission, and (d) controlled according to the Commission's agenda and terms of reference - has little in common with UK democracy. **Alternative view:** The EU does not have a different view of democracy. However, it does acknowledge a so-called "democratic deficit", and this is one area where reform could be likely and should be fought for by remaining in the EU.	

C. Benefits of leaving: *soft/indirect*

10. Ending societal breakdown There is plentiful evidence that large-scale immigration into the UK (now the most overcrowded country in the EU), from 27 other countries, has resulted in a much overcrowded UK society. It has meant a general fight for limited space and resources. And there are problems of absorption, assimilation, language, social cohesion, and acceptance of UK values and norms. Some of this is good, in giving a more diverse society and greater synergy. But much is not good, and it's forced on us. Many UK citizens see these things as changing the nature of UK society, and as the breakdown and erosion of UK society. **Alternative view:** Any so-called breakdown in UK society is purely a matter of opinion. Demographic experts say that the UK could accommodate another 15 million people without too much difficulty.	

Other *soft/indirect* benefits of leaving?
Put them and score them here

D. Benefits of leaving: *hard/direct*

1. No more contributions to the EU Budget The UK's net contribution to the EU Budget is now approaching £20 billion annually, which is likely to grow as poorer countries waiting to join, such as Turkey, come into the EU. This will be an early saving if the UK leaves the EU. **Alternative view:** The UK's contribution to the EU Budget is only a fraction of UK GDP/GNI (Gross Domestic Product or Gross National Income). Considering all the benefits of the UK remaining in the EU, our budget contribution is a bargain.	

D. Benefits of leaving: *hard/direct*

---

2. No more demands for Budget top-ups
The *European Commission* is well-known for (a) being very wasteful, (b) being very generous with its salaries, attendance allowances, expense accounts without receipts, office allowances, and pensions, and (c) its account books almost never having been signed off by its own *Court of Auditors*.

And EU MEPs are paid much more than UK MPs.

The *Committee of the Regions* is well-known for pouring money into extravagant, white elephant projects, and there have been problems of sleaze and defalcation of funds.

When the EU runs short of money it can demand further EU Budget contribution top-ups, as it did in demanding a further £1.7 billion from the UK in 2014.

Such top-up demands would cease if the UK were to leave the EU.

Alternative view: Top-up demands are not a regular occurrence every year, and the problem of sleaze with the Committee of the Regions is being addressed. The European Commission is also aware of the criticisms about spending and has put in place measures to correct the situation.

D. Benefits of leaving: *hard/direct*

---

3. Protective tariffs gone – lower shop prices
The reason for the UK joining the EU in 1973, or the EEC as it was then, was for free trade, mostly the avoidance of import duties or tariffs, which were as high as 40%.

Due to the efforts of the World Trade Organisation (WTO), these are now down to almost zero, which is the aim. The original reason for joining the EU has gone.

But on some things, like fruit (6.9%), shoes and clothing (11.6%), cereals (28.6%), dairy products (48.5%), meat (49.6%), cars (8.5%) the EU still imposes fairly high protective tariffs. This means higher prices in the showrooms and shops.

Leaving would mean lower prices on things like these. We wouldn't be paying EU protective tariffs on goods from outside the EU

Alternative view: As tariff rates come down around the world, and as the EU makes FTAs with other countries, high EU rates such as these will also come down.

The EU presently has free trade agreements with about 27 countries, with others in the pipeline.

D. Benefits of leaving: *hard/direct*

---

4. Reduced VAT: lower shop prices
VAT (Value Added Tax) is an *EU* sales tax, controlled by the EU. It was introduced when the UK joined the EEC (now the EU) in 1973. It is collected by HMRC on behalf of the *European Commission*.

A proportion of VAT tax receipts are sent to the EU.

The UK government's *Office for Budget Responsibility* (OBR) estimates that the VAT proportion sent to the EU will increase by about one-third over the next few years, to about £3 billion annually.

It is known that the EU aims to get rid of zero-rated items on food, children's clothing, books, newspapers & magazines, and medical prescription supplies. This will likely mean price increases in the shops on these things if the UK remains in the EU.

Alternative view: It's not certain that zero rating would end. Things are more likely to stay the same.
Taxes go up, never down, and it's unlikely that VAT would ever be reduced, no matter whether the UK is in or out of the EU. And it's only a very small proportion of VAT that goes to the EU.

D. Benefits of leaving: *hard/direct*

5. Cutting the costs of the EU Single Market EU Single Market regulatory compliance costs and bureaucracy apply to everyone *across the economy as a whole*, whether exporting to the EU or not. They apply to the NHS, local councils, government departments, local stores, clubs, pubs, sole traders, and businesses that do no exporting. They apply to everyone. There have been a few attempts to quantify the costs of the EU Single Market, and they are all in the tens of billions of pounds. It has been estimated by a former EU Commissioner, Gunter Verhuegen (who has since fallen from grace), that the *costs* of the EU Single Market versus the *benefits* across the EU are about 4:1. For the UK it has been estimated by Lea and Binley as about 2.5:1. There is also the *invisible* cost of displacing *productive* activity with *non*-productive activity - across the economy as a whole - with negative impact on economic activity. **Alternative view:** Many Single Market regulations would still apply even if the UK were not part of the EU, and the costs of the Single Market are grossly exaggerated.	

D. Benefits of leaving: *hard/direct*

---

6. Banished CAP – lower food prices
Agricultural policies for the EU as a whole under the *Common Agricultural Policy* (CAP) make food prices in the shops and supermarkets higher. It's been estimated by OXFAM and the OECD that this comes out at about £20 per week per family.

This should be no surprise, as the basic aim of the CAP has always been protective import duties against food products from outside the EU. This not only makes the cost of imported food from outside the EU more expensive in the shops. It also hurts poorer countries who produce cheaper food but which have to overcome the EU's protective import duty/tariff barriers.

Alternative view: Even though you might think that leaving the EU and getting rid of the CAP might give lower prices in the shops and supermarkets, there is no guarantee that it would actually happen. Real, genuine price reductions seldom happen; retailers have to keep profits up.

Besides, import tariffs are coming down, including those of the EU.

Also, FTAs are being struck by the EU with more countries, bringing down the cost of food imported from outside the EU.

D. Benefits of leaving: *hard/direct*

---

7. Banished CFP – regained fishing wealth
The Common Fisheries Policy (CFP) has resulted in
the decimation of Scottish, Welsh, N. Ireland, and
English fishing communities and, in spite of reforms,
still large-scale waste, inflexibility, and depletion of a
natural and rich food resource.

80 per cent of EU catch is in what used to be UK
waters. This could be regained.

The United Nations Law of the Sea of 1994 recognises
Exclusive Economic Zones, giving countries exclusive
fishing zones up to 200 miles from their shore lines or
the median point between countries.

Upon leaving the EU a new act of Parliament would
supersede the 1972 European Communities Act
(which got us into the EEC), saying "any provisions of
the European Communities Act notwithstanding" -
enabling the restoration of fishing grounds.

Alternative view: When the UK gave up its fishing
grounds to the EU on joining in 1973, it was not a good
thing. However, it is now history. CFP has now been
reformed. And it is unlikely after so many years that
the UK would have any residual legal claim over its
former fishing grounds.

D. Benefits of leaving: *hard/direct*

8. Ending costs of Working Time Directive Due to extra staffing costs the EU's Working Time Directive (WTD) is said to cost the NHS *millions* of pounds annually. It is estimated by *Open Europe*, (a think tank committed to a "slimmed-down, outward looking, and dynamic EU"), that the WTD costs the UK as whole more than £4 *billion* annually. Leaving should result in a large saving and a more sensible yet fair scheme, beginning with the NHS. **Alternative view:** The WTD is now well-entrenched, and unravelling it would be a logistical nightmare. There is no guarantee that trying to do this would result in a better scheme.

D. Benefits of leaving: *hard/direct*

9. Regained rights to make FTAs As a member of the European Union the UK is legally barred from making its own free (bilateral) trade agreements (FTAs). As shown by the success enjoyed by countries with much smaller economies such as Switzerland, Australia, New Zealand, and Singapore, made with major economies such as China, Japan, and India, this is a major *opportunity cost* for the UK. It demonstrates that being free to make its own FTA deals would unleash major opportunities in exports and jobs for the UK. Leaving the EU would also enable the UK to have its own seat on the WTO, as do most other countries in the world, and be able to represent itself directly and effectively. **Alternative view:** This would come at a cost, because the UK would (a) need to rebuild the trade negotiation skills it gave up to the EU, and/or buy in these skills, (b) rebuild its commercial consul staffing around the world, and (c) re-negotiate and replace the present 27 EU FTAs. Also, there is no way the UK could get better trade deals than the EU.	

D. Benefits of leaving: *hard/direct*

10. Not being dragged down by the Eurozone The Eurozone has been stagnating for a decade and, according to the IMF, there appears little prospect of change. Several counties, France, Italy, Portugal, and Greece, have dangerously high debt levels. There might be assurances that the UK does not have to commit to ever-close union with the Eurozone. But the UK would still be a member of the EU club, and the UK taxpayer would still have *joint and several liability* for all EU debts, not only for country bailouts, but also for insolvency bailouts of the European Central Bank and European Investment Bank. So there is a risk of the UK having to contribute to big bailouts that quite likely could occur. Leaving the EU would eliminate the risk. **Alternative view:** The UK government has sought assurances that the UK would not be responsible for any contributions to bailouts since it is not, nor does it wish to be, part of the Eurozone. This was agreed at the summit of EU leaders in Feb. 2016.

D. Benefits of leaving: *hard/direct*

11. Property/rental price rises contained According to the Migration Observatory at Oxford University, about half of all new government housing is needed for EU migrants. This displaces UK citizens. It also means that overall demand for housing is greater than supply, which pushes up prices and values. Building more and more housing cannot continue to be the answer as the UK is not a big country in size. Leaving the EU would put a cap on large people inflows to the UK, and should slow down the rate of increase in rental and property prices. **Alternative view:** House building at present does not use enough brown-field sites due to government restrictions. If these were lifted the problem would be alleviated.	

D. Benefits of leaving: *hard/direct*

---

12. In-work and child benefits: down
If UK or EU citizens have a wage that gives them less than the legally-required level of income they can claim in-work benefits

And with low wages acceptable by many migrants, and UK employers often preferring them for this reason, it pushes down wage levels for everyone, which results in the need for higher in-work benefits overall

The Department of Work and Pensions had 266,000 EU migrants applying for in-work benefits in 2014.

Also, migrants can claim child benefits equally with UK citizens, which is about £20 per week per child.

Alternative view: As the *Living Wage* comes into operation, which is roughly 30 per cent higher per hour than the Minimum Wage, this will increase wages for many migrants, and should largely resolve the problem.

Most incoming migrants work and pay taxes, and are entitled to child benefits as much as anyone else. In any case, only a small proportion of migrants claim child benefits.

Other *hard/direct* benefits of leaving?
Put them and score them here

C JAMES BACON

PART II: ADDITIONAL READING

- How it all changed when EEC became EU

- The EU economic argument: five key points

- What's the EU Single Market?

- Immigration, open borders, free movement

- Liberty, democracy, sovereignty – and the EU

How It All Changed when EEC Became EU

Life for the UK citizen began to change when the European Economic Community became the European Union with the 1992 Maastricht Treaty.

Maastricht amended the 1957 Treaty of Rome. This was amended and strengthened by the Amsterdam Treaty of 1997 with its Schengen Agreement, the Social Chapter in 1999, the Nice Treaty of 2002, and the Lisbon Treaty of 2007.

Maastricht and its amending treaties took the UK and other member countries from being in a free-trade customs union and headed for ever-closer union in a United States of Europe.

Background

Before the United Kingdom joined what was the *European Economic Community* (EEC) in 1973, laws affecting the UK were initiated and enacted by the UK Parliament.

Since then the Scottish Parliament, Welsh Assembly, and Northern Ireland Assembly have come into being, providing for devolved powers and greater sovereignty (self-government) for these parts of the UK.

The UK Government may now push devolution further, to major cities and parts of the UK, and to England itself.

But joining the EEC, and especially when it became the *European Union* (EU) in 1992, took the UK in the opposite direction.

From devolution in one direction, it went to centralisation and reduced sovereignty in the other.

At the beginning, the EEC required the UK to give up only part of its national sovereignty (for example over its fishing grounds), in exchange for being part of the 'Common Market'.

It was presented and seen by almost everyone as a *free trade* issue – opening up Western Europe to UK trade and vice versa by eliminating tariffs and trade barriers.

They are disappearing now, but at the time tariffs were as high as 40%.

The political aim was there to be seen in the 1957 Treaty of Rome and even before, but unseen in 1973 by most members of parliament.

Or if the political aim *was* seen by some (as it was by PM Edward Heath), it was not shared with the general public.

When EEC became EU: the main changes

- The 1992 Maastricht Treaty with its amending treaties and especially Lisbon, changed the European Economic Community (EEC) to the European Union (EU). And it legally made the EU a country in its own right, sovereign above its member states.

- The most basic change was that Maastricht gave much bigger scope for the UK's law-making authority and UK courts to be over-ridden by the law-making powers of the European Union in EU *competences*, i.e. the EU has exclusive power to make law in these areas, with the UK Parliaments and Assemblies made redundant.

  The change may have been noticed by people coming up against official restrictions, and by small businesses affected by the cost and nature of new EU regulations, in some cases forcing them out of business. But, very often, the EU itself was hidden and unseen, behind new UK national agencies doing the work for it.

- The Maastricht Treaty brought in the *Economic & Monetary Union* (EMU) with the aim of integrating member countries' economic, fiscal, and monetary policies.

- Possibly the most visible change was that Maastricht brought in a common *Euro currency* and *Eurozone*, and with it the *European Central Bank* (ECB) in Frankfurt, setting a common interest rate for all member countries.

- Another big change was *Schengen* becoming EU law, making for open borders in the EU.

- The 1999 *Social Chapter* was brought in as an annex to Maastricht, with powers for more EU involvement in the daily life and work of people.

- The 2007 Lisbon Treaty gave the EU 50 more competences (exclusive law-making powers). At the same time it removed 55 rights of veto while bringing in qualified majority voting.

  The aim was to prevent a member country such as the UK blocking ever-closer union, even where there was a conflict with UK vital interests.

- The EU also took over responsibility for a major part of the foreign affairs and diplomatic representation of member states, in a new *European External Action Service*, now represented in most countries around the world.

- The EU also increased its powers over a large part of Justice and Home Affairs (JHA).

- It established a *Committee of the Regions,* giving the EU authority to directly involve itself with UK regions, by-passing UK Government authority and providing funding directly to the regions (having collected these funds from the UK govt.).

- It brought in *EU 'citizenship'* – anyone who comes to live, study, or work in the UK from any member country can vote in UK elections and is entitled to the same social, health, and unemployment benefits as UK citizens.

- Symbolising EU citizenship were EU passports and EU driving licenses, day-to-day symbols of national (UK) citizenship coming under EU citizenship.

- And it brought in an EU flag and an EU anthem (adapted from Beethoven's Ode to Joy) – further symbols of the EU as a nation-state.

- Like Bastille Day, St Patrick's Day, St Andrews Day, St David's Day, and St George's Day, the EU brought in its own national day, the 9th of May.

- When *EEC* became *EU* it went from *inter*-governmental co-operation to *supra*-governmental (above government) control, with the European Commission as the executive power exercising much of this control.

- The European Commission is supported in its executive control and aim of ever-closer union by:

   a. The European Court of Justice (ECJ) decisions over-riding UK law and UK courts. There is no appeal. It is not a neutral court.

   b. The Committee of Permanent Reps (Coreper), serving the Council of Ministers. Coreper prepares the agendas and oversees 250 committees and working parties.

Maastricht was a milestone in what began as a free trade customs union with the Treaty of Rome, aiming to become one country in a United States of Europe.

The EU Economic Argument: Five Key Points

- Regulations and productivity

- Growing yet declining

- Business is business

- The bigness problem

- The UK: An FTA hub

Regulations and productivity

EU regulations and bureaucracy are said to be "crushing Europe", and weighing heavily on the UK economy.

There have been a few attempts to quantify the costs of the EU Single Market, and they are all in the tens of billions of pounds.

For example, it was estimated by former EU Commissioner Gunter Verhuegen that the costs of the EU Single Market are about four times the benefits.

If the UK were *not* a member country most of this regulatory compliance and bureaucracy cost would not apply.

Yet the UK would still enjoy access to the Single Market. See: *EU Single Market Cost vs Benefit*

The burden & cost of regulatory compliance and bureaucracy in

management time, people, IT systems, administration, training, record-keeping, and reporting

across the economy as a whole

Benefit

Market size and process efficiencies

across the economy as a whole

Benefit for *exporters* (5% UK cos.)

The *invisible* cost of displacing *productive* activity with *non-*productive activity

across the economy as a whole.

EU Single Market cost v. benefit: net positive or net negative?

The conclusion is that leaving the EU would likely lead to a significant decrease in costs for business and government across the UK economy, and a net increase in *productivity*.

This is important, because:

> *Productivity is fundamental to the economic performance of any country.*

And

> *Lack of productivity is a key reason why the Eurozone continues to stagnate.*

C. Northcote Parkinson showed some time ago (*Parkinson's Law*, 1956), that bureaucracy is a blessing for civil servants, since it creates more work and greater rewards - and everyone works (or not) according to rewards.

This may explain why the UK agencies that have sprung up to do EU work often gold-plate regulations coming from Brussels (like turning three pages of EU instructions for using step-ladders into 21 pages).

So if the outcome of the EU Referendum is that the UK should leave, then life after the EU will involve an adjustment process that will need to include a question:

1. *Does an EU regulation need to be retained?*

2. *If so, how could it be made more efficient & effective?*

3. *If not, how might it best/fairly be phased out?*

But it will need the pro-active support of UK civil servants, and a different focus.

There would be more profitable work in export promotion and international trade development, with a UK able to promote its own trade interests in free trade agreements with other countries.

Growing yet declining

The EU has been growing in the number of countries but declining economically for about a decade. Since the relative value of any economy can generally be evaluated over the course of time from the price of its currency, this decline can be seen in the fall of the Euro.

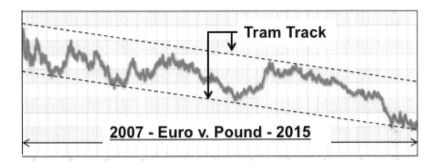

The Pound has fallen against the Euro since the beginning of 2016, due to uncertainty about the outcome of the Referendum, and markets *hate* uncertainty.

It has also been due to financial institutions talking down the pound, which is a fairly common big money tactic in currency markets, the aim being to profit from the fear/greed psyche of 'the herd'.

Tram track analysis shows that, once the outcome of the referendum is known, the Euro is likely to fall against the Pound.

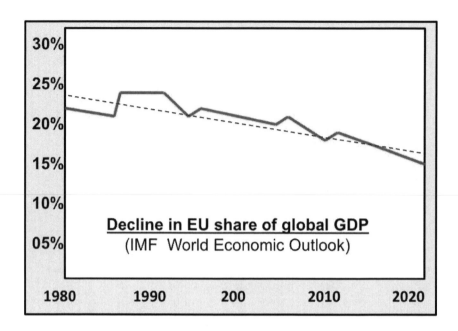

And in the decline of UK exports to the EU.

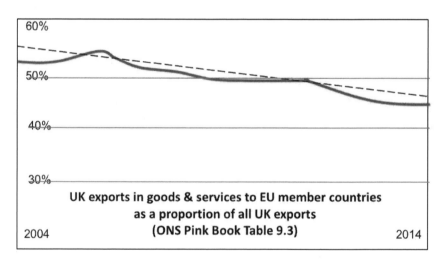

A comparison of GDP growth between the EU and the Commonwealth may reveal where potential for trade lies.

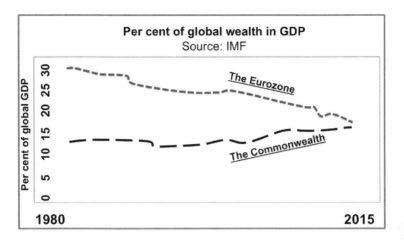

The International Monetary Fund (IMF) has forecast that the EU growth picture is unlikely to change much in the next few years. Instead, the economic performance of the Eurozone may get worse. For example:

- The very high debt levels of some EU member countries (France, Italy, Portugal, and Greece) is so serious that before long there may need to be large bailouts.

  If the UK is still in the EU, and even though not in the Eurozone, it may be forced, directly or indirectly, to pay a share of these bailouts.

- Other, poorer countries are waiting to join the EU (Turkey and others), with a total of about 100 million population.

  If the UK is still in the EU, it will likely be forced to accept more EU citizens as economic migrants, with entitlement to benefit payouts.

  These countries will also need infrastructure spending, and the UK will need to be a major contributor.

If, therefore, the UK is in a growing EU that is declining economically, then it is likely to be adversely affected.

Business is business

If the UK were to leave the European Union, exports to the EU and the jobs that go with them will not be much affected by the imposition of protective EU tariffs..

This is because the UK *imports* much more from other EU member countries than it *exports* to them.

The UK is the EU's biggest customer - bigger even than the United States.

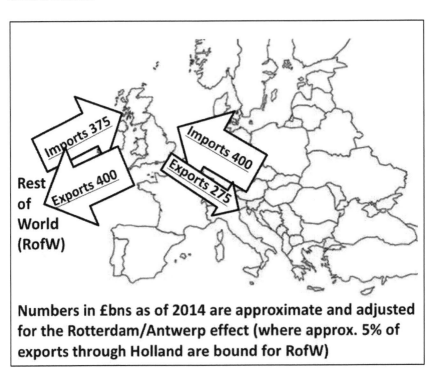

Rest
of
World
(RofW)

Imports 375
Exports 400
Imports 400
Exports 275

Numbers in £bns as of 2014 are approximate and adjusted for the Rotterdam/Antwerp effect (where approx. 5% of exports through Holland are bound for RofW)

If the UK leaves the EU, and given that the UK is the EU's biggest customer, it can be assumed that a favourable free trade agreement (FTA) would be struck.

Furthermore:

- Tariffs would stay much the same, and then become less.

- There would be access to the EU Single Market at least as good as any other country with which the EU has an FTA.

- Since there is no requirement with other countries having FTAs with the EU (for example Mexico, Chile, and South Korea), to comply with the EU's free movement of people for access to the EU Single Market – then neither would there be any such requirement for the UK.

- Possibly not being consulted on EU Single Market regulations would be of little importance.

Most importantly, no jobs would be lost on either side, for the UK or the EU.

For example:

- German and French car companies would not want to lose out to Japanese Korean, and indeed British car manufacturers. Mercedes, BMW, Audi, Porsche, Peugeot, Citroen, and Renault would make strong representations to their governments that their large sales to the UK should not be put at a disadvantage.

- French, Italian, and Spanish wine producers would not want to lose out to Australian, New Zealand, South African, and Chilean wine producers.

- Italian, Spanish, and Portuguese shoe and boot manufacturers will not want to lose out to Chinese and Vietnamese shoe and boot manufacturers.

These and other EU exporters will not want protective tariffs (import duties) imposed on their large exports to the UK, because:

Business is business.

So the UK could expect amicable, quid pro quo arrangements to be made. Jobs will not be put at risk on either side.

This is in spite of a *factoid* still circulating that the UK will lose millions of jobs if it leaves the EU.

This is something that is seldom if ever explained or justified. It simply keeps getting repeated.

The bigness problem

The European Union has become too big and complex, and so has become inward looking, poorly managed, wasteful, autocratic, sleazy, over-powerful, mired in the past, and costly.

But the bigness problem isn't just the EU.

It applies as a systemic risk and cost for *all* organisations both government and non-government, as shown in *Why bigness costs.*

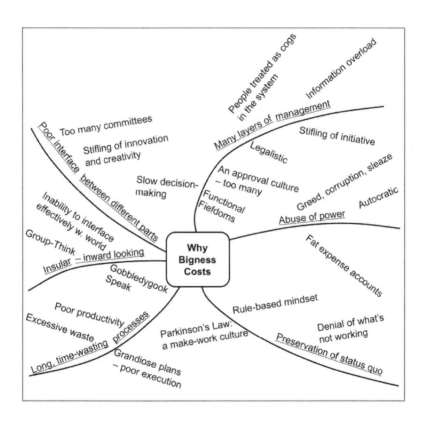

The bigness problem is due to any kind of government, political, or business organisation being a *system* for a *purpose*, and problems come in when there is *bigness* with *complexity* in the system.

The following page shows the forces for limited government versus big government. It translates fairly well to the EU.

The bigness problem is based on the following, *Systems Thinking* principle:

Every business, government, or other kind of human organisation,
*   -   as a system –*
has a maximum size & complexity, beyond which the organisation
becomes an increasingly non-effective and non-viable 'dinosaur'
in pursuing its purpose, leading almost inevitably to its demise.

But there may be exceptions or delays in bigness leading to demise if it is:

- *A simple organisation*

- *Ring-fenced by subsidy or status as an essential (govt.) department.*

- *Protected by physical and/or psychological force of some kind.*

- *Partitioned into self-governing units.*

- *Reformed by some traumatic event.*

Becoming much smaller, and giving up much of its centralised political power might come about in the EU through some traumatic event, such as member countries leaving.
If not, its destiny is extinction.

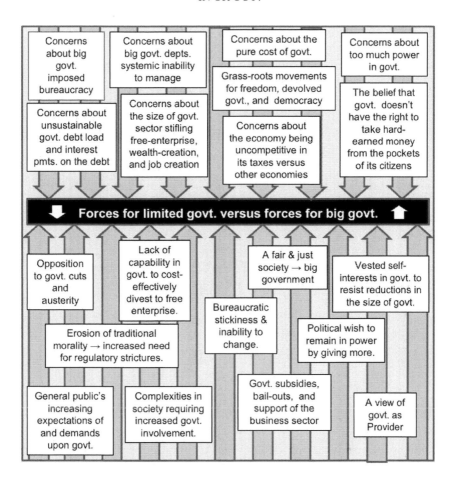

The UK: An FTA hub (and the Swiss FTA success story)

Being in the EU trading bloc has prevented the UK from dealing on its own merit and on its own behalf with other countries or groups of countries. For example, with the 50-plus member nations of the Commonwealth such as India, Canada, Australia, New Zealand, and South Africa. This has been a big lost-opportunity cost.

Being in the EU, the UK is barred from making its own trade deals. It has to be represented by the EU Trade Commissioner.

So the UK has no seat on the World Trade Organisation (WTO). It is taken by the EU in representing all EU member countries. We're not allowed to speak for ourselves.

Cutting loose, the UK would be free to make free, (bilateral) trade agreements (FTAs), as do for example Switzerland, Australia, India, and Mexico.

Each of these countries are FTA *hubs*, since they have consistent *rules of origin* in all their FTAs, which clearly state the criteria used to define where a product was made.

The UK could develop itself into being such a *hub*, which would attract greater foreign direct investment (FDI).

And the UK could well follow *The Swiss FTA Success Story* on the following pages.

But how and why could the UK do better representing itself, rather than being represented by a big player EU representing the UK and 27 other member countries?

1. Motivation: the EU can never be as well motivated in representing each of 28 member countries, as a country such as the UK can be in representing itself.

2. The EU cannot very well *represent* 28 member countries, all with different economies and different strengths. The UK does not, for example, have a large shoe industry to

promote and protect like Italy, or large wine production like France, or diamond processing like The Netherlands. But it does have a Scottish and Northern Irish whiskey industry (for example), which it could better promote by and for itself.

3. The EU does not give much priority to *business services* (e.g. insurance, banking, accounting, legal services, wealth management, foreign exchange, and management consulting) in its FTAs, which is a strength area for the UK. Compared with *Swiss* FTAs, EU FTAs hardly ever include services. Swiss FTAs *almost always* do. This represents another lost-opportunity cost for the UK while it remains a member of the EU.

4. The UK can itself negotiate free trade agreements (FTAs) much quicker than the EU (which has a reputation for moving with glacial slowness), so bringing in swifter economic benefits.

5. The UK already has good, international relationships, as for example with Commonwealth countries and the United States, on which it can build.

6. The UK is a much bigger country in population, GDP, and trade than Switzerland, Norway, Iceland, and other countries which have been successful, in spite of their smaller size, in striking FTAs with very large countries around the world, such as China, Japan, and the EU itself.

7. See Jonathan Lindsell in the Sources section at the back of the book: *Lessons from Switzerland: How might Britain go about business outside the EU?*

The Swiss FTA Success Story

Excerpts from the web site of Swiss Economic Affairs
(Swiss population 8.2 million vs UK 65 million)

Switzerland has a large network of free (bilateral)
trade agreements, or FTAs (BTAs).

Switzerland normally concludes its FTAs together with its
partners Norway, Iceland and Liechtenstein, in the European
Free Trade Association (EFTA).

But it also enters into FTAs outside the EFTA, as for example,
with Japan and China.

Switzerland's prosperity depends on international trade in
goods and services. Consequently, the constant improvement
of access to foreign markets is a core objective of Swiss
foreign economic policy.

The best way to achieve this is the multilateral approach within
the framework of the WTO.

At the same time, a growing number of countries are entering
into FTAs, as a way to complement ongoing multilateral trade
liberalisation.

By entering into FTAs, Switzerland aims to provide its
companies with access to international markets that is at least
equivalent to the market access conditions enjoyed by its most
important competitors (such as the EU, the USA and Japan).

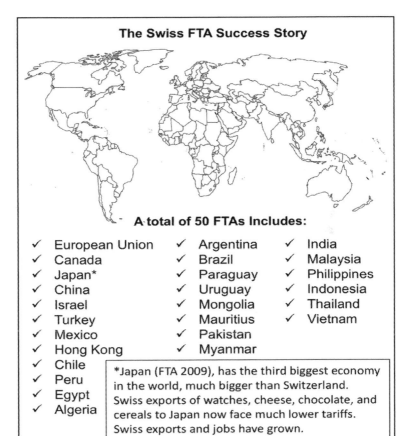

The Swiss FTA Success Story

A total of 50 FTAs Includes:

- ✓ European Union
- ✓ Canada
- ✓ Japan*
- ✓ China
- ✓ Israel
- ✓ Turkey
- ✓ Mexico
- ✓ Hong Kong
- ✓ Chile
- ✓ Peru
- ✓ Egypt
- ✓ Algeria

- ✓ Argentina
- ✓ Brazil
- ✓ Paraguay
- ✓ Uruguay
- ✓ Mongolia
- ✓ Mauritius
- ✓ Pakistan
- ✓ Myanmar

- ✓ India
- ✓ Malaysia
- ✓ Philippines
- ✓ Indonesia
- ✓ Thailand
- ✓ Vietnam

*Japan (FTA 2009), has the third biggest economy in the world, much bigger than Switzerland. Swiss exports of watches, cheese, chocolate, and cereals to Japan now face much lower tariffs. Swiss exports and jobs have grown.

Note:
The European Union has about 27 FTAs in force, with others planned.

What's the EU Single Market?

1. Single market vs customs union.
2. The EU web site article.
3. Cost vs benefit: member countries.
4. Cost vs benefit: non-member countries.
5. Having a voice: UK influence

1. Single market vs customs union

It may be useful to clarify the distinction between the EU *Single Market* and the EU *Customs Union*:

The EU Customs Union means: no *internal* tariffs (customs duties) between EU member countries, and protective *external* tariffs against imports from outside the EU into any member country.

In comparison, the EU *Single Market* is about being free of *non-tariff* trade barriers or Technical Barriers to Trade (TBTs) by harmonising standards and procedures for goods and services.

To a large extent the EU Single Market is about meeting *CE* standard on physical products, similar to ISO or British Kite Mark standard.

For example, it might deal with safety specifications in car brakes, eco design of energy-related products, the required shape of a cucumber, and EU rules and regulations in selling cabbages.

But for member countries the EU Single Market is also about *work practices* such as the Working Time Directive.

Being free of TBTs (as compared with a situation where different countries have different standards and procedures) - makes it easier and more efficient to buy and sell within the EU.

For exporters, importers, and distributors based and operating in the EU, it becomes virtually one, big, domestic market. It reduces time and cost for companies, and expands choice for consumers.

Increasingly, the European Commission gets its standards and procedures from global bodies - such as the World Trade Organisation (WTO), UN Economic Commission for Europe (UNECE), International Standards Organisation, (ISO), in banking the Basel Committee, or in food standards Codex Alimentarius.

There are 162 member countries in the WTO with 21 waiting to join, but the UK is not one of them. Like the other 27 EU member countries, it is represented by the Trade Commissioner of the European Commission.

In this sense the EU is a middleman, passing down standards and procedures from global bodies.

2. The EU web site article

In the EU Commission web site article *One Market without Borders it says:*

> *EU citizens can study, live, shop, work, and retire in any EU country – and enjoy products from all over Europe. Hundreds of technical, legal, and bureaucratic barriers to free trade and free movement between the EU's member countries have been abolished.*
>
> *As a result, companies have expanded their operations. The competition has brought prices down, and given consumers more choice.*

As the article says, the abolition of these barriers has helped companies expand operations, enabling economies of scale and lower prices.

However, there is a downside. With product standardisation there is a comparison with Henry Ford's "You can have any colour as long as it's black".

In other words it may *limit* choice, and tends to favour large-scale production by multinational companies - even though small businesses may succeed in niche areas. It also tends to limit competition with these large multinationals, many of whom lobby the European Commission from offices in Brussels.

But the EU is first and foremost a Customs Union, side-by-side with it being a Single Market.

The downside of the EU Customs Union is that it is protectionist against trade from *outside* the EU.

It protects certain industries such as French farming and Italian shoes by imposing import tariffs (and some import tariffs are quite hefty) on these products from countries outside the EU.

This means that prices on products imported from outside the EU are higher in the shops than they would be otherwise.

The Commission's article then says:

- *Fragmented national tax systems impede market integration and undermine efficiency.*

- *Separate national markets still exist for financial services , energy, and transport.*

- *The services sector is lagging behind the goods market.*

"Fragmented national tax systems" is *EuroSpeak* - meaning that taxes need to be the same across the EU. It's a key objective in a *United States of Europe*.

It means, for example, that if the rate of income tax, corporate tax, or sales tax in France is high, then it needs to be just as high in the UK, otherwise it *"impedes market integration and undermines efficiency"*.

The alternative view is that national governments need to be free to compete against each other in their tax regimes in attracting business and investment, and in responding to taxpayer demands for lower taxes.

The Republic of Ireland, for example, has been hugely successful in attracting multinational computer software companies, with Dublin and Galway now global software hubs, and with many hi-tech jobs having been created.

Ireland has a corporate tax rate of 12.5% to 25%, compared to a corporate tax rate of 33% for France and 30% for Germany. In the UK it is 20% and going down to 18% by 2020.

As for the "services sector lagging behind" in the article, this has hurt the UK. The EU is oriented to physical products and manufacturing, more than services.

3. Cost vs benefit: member countries
So the underlying _benefit_ of the European Single Market for exporters based _within_ member countries is one set of standards and procedures for exports to any and all other member countries.

Against this is the _cost_ of compliance, needless and often nonsensical regulations, and bureaucracy generally.

The Working Time Directive, for example, which the European Commission made part of the Single Market, is said to cost the NHS alone millions of pounds annually – with knock-on impacts on UK health if not lives (as for example in the provision of adequateambulance services).

And of course as a whole, EU Single Market compliance and bureaucracy costs the UK economy much more.
So the question is:

Which is greater, _cost_ or _benefit_ of the EU Single Market?

- If you're an _exporter_ in an EU member country, exporting to another member country, there are costs and benefits, with the benefits assumed to be greater than the costs.

- If you're _not_ an exporter in an EU member country there are costs but no benefits. You have to comply with not only Single Market but _all_ EU rules and regulations; they apply to all, across the entire economy.

In other words, for a member country such as the UK, the _cost_ of compliance, needless and often nonsensical regulations, and bureaucracy with the Single Market, and indeed EU regulations as a whole, apply to:

Companies that export, companies that don't export, local councils, the NHS, central government, plumbers, electricians, hairdressers, sole traders, and individuals.

They apply across the board to every area of business and society, if the country is a member of the European Union.

There have been a few studies estimating the cost v. benefit of the EU Single Market for member countries, and the costs as a whole are said to outweigh the benefits as a whole by a ratio of at least 2:1, with some estimates a lot more.

This is illustrated in *EU Single Market: Member Country Cost vs Benefit*.

It illustrates the *benefit* for *exporters* in an EU member country, exporting to other member countries in the EU

versus

The *cost* of the EU Single Market for a *member country as a whole*.

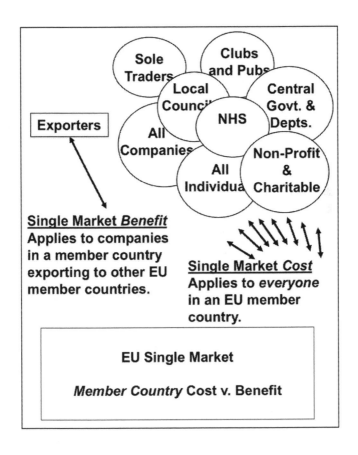

4. Cost vs benefit: non-member countries

It is not necessary for a country to belong to the European Union to enjoy the benefits of the EU Single Market.

Exporters based in countries who are *not* members of the EU, and export to the EU – enjoy most of the benefits.

This means that exporters exporting to the EU from outside need to meet EU requirements, as for example in meeting *CE* product standards. However, it might mean some added paperwork, unless there is a free trade agreement (FTA) in place with the EU.

And for any exporter operating from a country not a member of the EU - the country might not be consulted in defining Single Market standards and procedures.

However, it appears likely that *WTO*-led harmonisation will take on greater influence and importance in coming years, displacing EU harmonisation of standards and procedures.

In other words, consultation at EU-level is becoming less important.

The cost vs benefit scenario for *non*-member countries is illustrated in: EU Single Market *Non-Member Country* Cost v. Benefit.

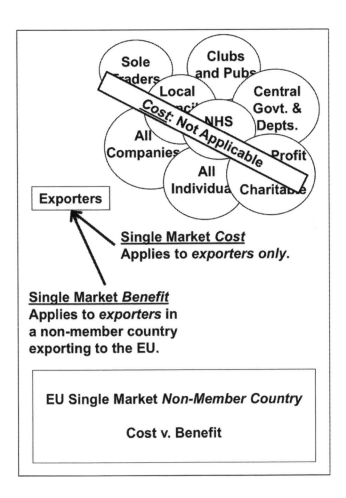

Single Market *Cost*
Applies to *exporters only*.

Single Market *Benefit*
Applies to *exporters* in
a non-member country
exporting to the EU.

EU Single Market *Non-Member Country*

Cost v. Benefit

To clarify and summarise:

1. If the UK were not a member of the EU it would enjoy most of the benefits of its single market, but avoid the costs.

2. An EU standard or procedure may be based on an international standard, such as WTO, UNECE, ISO or any one of about 50 international standards organisations.

3. If a company is exporting a product to the EU from a non-member country, it might meet the EU Single Market requirement through the international standard.

4. If the EU has a FTA with a country it will include reduction if not elimination of protective customs tariffs and TBTs, and may include consultation. This would likely apply to the UK if it leaves the EU – since the UK is the EU's biggest customer.

5. It's a scenario made more likely with *WTO* laws making it illegal to discriminate in trade against other countries, and by *EU* laws requiring the EU to maintain friendly trade relations with neighbouring non-member countries.

Why is it, then (since you don't really need to be in the EU to have access to the EU's Single Market) that some big, multinational companies are in favour of remaining in the EU?

Possible reasons are as follows:

- A *lack of awareness* that you don't need to be in the EU to enjoy access to the Single Market.

- Not being aware of or concerned about the *cost* of Single Market and EU bureaucracy on *the whole* of the UK economy, and of it's indirect cost impact on all companies.

- A large multinational company finds that it has become comfortable and used to doing business with the EU and its way of operating – and *concern/fear of change*.

- Big companies having *big influence* with the European Commission, sitting in committees and working groups, and with tens of thousands of big company lobbyists based in Brussels.

- The EU is both a Single Market and a Customs Union, and the Customs Union imposes protective tariffs on anything imported into the EU (unless there is an FTA). Big companies would be *protected* against cheaper imported products – and this protection might disappear if the UK leaves the EU.

- Big companies benefit from the low, pressed-down wages resulting from large numbers of migrants willing to work for less. If the UK leaves the EU and mass immigration is replaced by controlled immigration, wages will tend to rise, meaning increases in wage bills.

5. Having a voice: UK influence.

Concerning any cost in not having a voice or influence on EU Single Market standards and procedures, and/or regulations and law-making of the European Union, the present influence of the UK in the EU is illustrated below.

The UK is 1 of 28 countries: 3.6%.

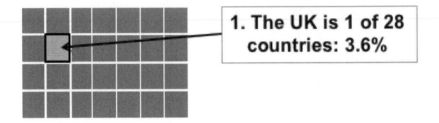

1. The UK is 1 of 28 countries: 3.6%

The EU outer circle in which the UK sits is shown below.

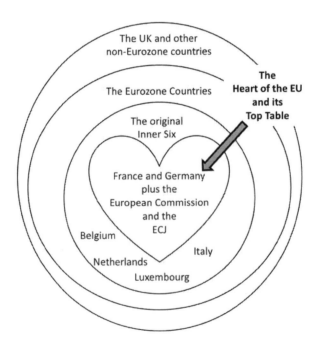

Since the UK joined the EU in 1973 (or the EEC as it then was), it has opposed about 55 regulations and has lost on each one. They have all become law.

An example where the UK's little influence in the EU was sharply shown was in the Working Time Directive (WTD).

The UK government objected strongly to the WTD because it was against UK vital interests (as for example in costing the NHS millions). But UK objections were overruled.

Another example is Tampon sales tax under VAT. The EU classifies these as luxury items, so they are *taxed* as luxury items.

EU regulations such as this over-ride UK laws. The UK has little or no influence.

1. Freedom of people: a right most cherished
2. Feasibility for the UK
3. Economic growth and impact on jobs
4. Discrimination
5. Truth vs fiction
6. EU Free Movement Directive 2004/038

Immigration, open borders, free movement

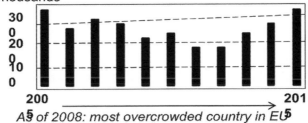

Net Migration Into the UK 2005 → 2015
Actual figures likely to exceed official ONS figures
13 Countries have joined the EU since 2004

Hundred
Thousands

As of 2008: most overcrowded country in EU

Including excerpts and comments from the
European Commission web site article:
*European Commission Upholds
Free Movement of People*

1. The free movement of people - a right most cherished

The article on the European Commission web site "European Commission Upholds Free Movement of People" was published before the 2015 jihadist attacks in France and Belgium, and before the migrant crisis.

The article begins with the statement that:

> *Free movement – or the ability to live, work and study anywhere in the Union – is the EU right most cherished by Europeans . . .*

But in reducing the *home country* unemployment problem the "right most cherished" leaves these countries with

- a lost generation of young people, and

- a hollowed-out gap of doctors, nurses, lawyers, tradesmen, and other professionals who are led to migrate.

And there have been problems with the NHS being forced to accept qualifications from any and all EU countries as being equal to UK qualifications.

2. Feasibility for the UK

The free movement of people is non-feasible for countries such as the UK, which is now the most overcrowded country in Europe, with England twice as densely populated as Germany, and four times as densely populated as France.

In England:

- Housing sites are being built across the green countryside. "Tied up in traffic" is common.
- Commuting trains are standing-room only.
- The NHS is overwhelmed and going broke.
- Police forces are stretched and "only half of crimes are solved".
- Secondary school places are "undeliverable".
- Doctor's surgeries are at "breaking point".
- Pollution is high (greatly decreased butterfly population being an indicator).

It's a society overcrowded, breaking down, and with a fight for limited space and resources.

Since 2004 the UK population increase, with 13 more countries joining the EU (and another seven countries including Turkey with 100 million total population waiting to join) - has been almost entirely due to immigration.

Yet official ONS figures are likely to be lower than actual, due to widespread abuse of student and visitor visas, illegal entries, and official miscounts.

For example, according to the Department for Work and Pensions, the International Passenger Survey figures used by the government counted 750,000 incoming migrants from June 2012 to June 2015. In comparison, nearly two million National Insurance numbers were given out to EU citizens; more than twice as many.

A further issue under the heading of feasibility is social mix and cohesion. With very large numbers of incoming migrants there is a problem of assimilation, national identity, norms and values, and acceptance of host country culture.

So that many people see such large-scale immigration as changing the nature of UK society, but not for the better.

With open borders throughout the EU criminals and jihadists enter and find their way to Western Europe (hence the 2015 attacks in Paris and Belgium).

And since border controls in Greece have broken down, it appears that everyone and anyone is waived through.

It's also reported that many are *economic* migrants, including those whose livelihoods have been taken away by EU fishing off African coasts.

However, although related, the migrant crisis is a separate issue from immigration, open borders, and free movement within the EU.

Economic growth and impact on jobs

The EU Commission article continues:

Free movement of citizens . . . is an integral component of the Single Market and a central element of its success: it stimulates economic growth by enabling people to travel and shop across borders.

Equally, the free movement of workers benefits not only the workers involved but also the Member States' economies, allowing for an efficient matching of skills with vacancies in the EU labour market.

But free movement of people may or may not stimulate economic growth. It may do the opposite if large numbers of incoming migrants have little skills and are reliant on welfare benefits.

And it is not necessary for the efficient matching of needed skills with vacancies, since this is commonly accomplished by countries having schemes of *controlled* immigration, as for example with the North American Free Trade Association (NAFTA).

Nor has free movement of people ever been part of the principle of *comparative economic advantage*.

But it is a source of cheap labour.

The following analysis shows how mass immigration into the UK has pressed down wages and led to job losses for UK citizens.

- The greatly increased supply of labour shifts the supply curve to the <u>right</u>.

- This presses down the price/cost of labour, from A to B, i.e. lower wages.

- The lower price of labour leads to increased demand for labour, from A to B, as it makes it cheaper to do things, make things, and buy things, albeit with increased economic activity.

- The greatly increased supply of labour also increases the competition for jobs, further forcing down wages.

- It forces wage-earners to accept lower wages, with jobs given to those who are prepared to work for less; foreign workers accustomed to much lower wages get the jobs and displace UK citizens from these jobs.

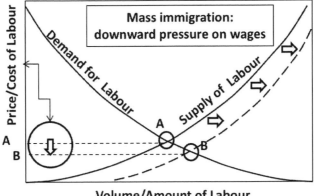

4. Discrimination

The EU Commission article continues:

Regulation No. 2011/492 details workers' rights to free movement and defines specific areas where discrimination on grounds of nationality is prohibited, in particular as regards: access to employment, working conditions, social and tax advantages, access to training, membership of trade unions, housing, and access to education for children . . .

Any restriction of foreign EU people's rights to all the rights and privileges enjoyed by a country's resident citizens is described as "discrimination".

But really, it is discrimination against a country's own citizens, who will be locked out of jobs, accommodation, access to NHS and social resources, and space in which to live and move around, all because demand exceeds supply.

It also discriminates against people from outside the EU who may have better skills (for example, nurses from the Phillipines)

A third issue with regulation 492/2011 is the common occurrence of EU migrants drawn/pulled to the UK due its benefits system and free health care.

There is no estimate of the full cost of benefits for migrants, but health tourism is reported to cost the NHS £600 million per year. It's a factor in forcing the NHS to breaking point.

So the pull factor in encouraging migrants from the poorer countries of the EU is strong. However, the biggest pull factor is the difference in wages, which is said to be six times the average wage rates in Romania and Poland.

This wage pull factor is set to become even stronger as the new and higher Living Wage comes in.

So more migrants shifts the demand curve for housing to the right – with knock on effect on the cost of housing/rentals.

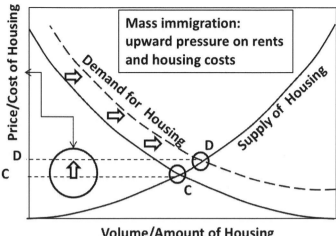

Volume/Amount of Housing

5. Truth vs Fiction

The article continues:

> *Labour mobility in the EU benefits not only the workers involved but also the Member States' economies. It benefits host countries because it allows companies to fill vacancies that would otherwise not be filled, and so produce goods and provide services that they would otherwise be unable to do.*

As before, other free trade areas such as NAFTA do not involve or require the free movement of people.

Also, the EU itself has FTAs with the about 27 countries, such as Algeria, Chile, Egypt, Israel, Mexico, Norway, South Africa, South Korea, and Turkey, and with none of these is there a requirement for the free movement of people.

The EU's *Fourth Freedom*, the free movement of people, does not, therefore, appear to be needed for any identifiable reason.

And there is little evidence that it "allows companies to fill vacancies that would not otherwise not be filled". It is equally valid to argue that it shuts out UK citizens from jobs.

So it appears that the EU's *Fourth Freedom*, the free movement of people, may have some other reason.

This other reason may be that of imposing the vision of one *demos* (one people) in a U.S. of Europe.

It goes all the way back to the founders' well-intentioned and understandable belief, tracing all the way back to before the First World War in 1914-1918 - that to prevent war there must be one European *demos*.

To encourage this there must be open borders, uncontrolled immigration, and free movement of people.

6. EU Free Movement Directive 2004/038

Finally, the EU web site article concludes:

> *. . . and it benefits citizens' countries of origin because it allows workers that would otherwise be less able to find jobs and so ensure financial support to their family back home and acquire skills and experience they would otherwise lack*
>
> *In The [1992] <u>Treaty of Maastricht</u>, the right to free movement was recognised for all EU citizens, irrespective of whether they are economically active or not as one of the fundamental freedoms conferred on them by EU law (Article 21 of the Treaty on the Functioning of the European Union).*
>
> *It goes to the heart of EU Citizenship.*

It is the Schengen Agreement (attached to the 1997 Amsterdam Treaty), which gives EU freedom of movement, from which the UK (and Ireland) has an opt-out.

But the UK is still, in effect, tied to Schengen, based on *EU Free Movement Directive 2004/038*. With this directive the UK is compelled to accept unrestricted immigration and provide full benefits to migrants from EU states.

Liberty, Democracy, Sovereignty - and the EU

Liberty:

Freedom of the *individual person* in living his/her life without undue government control or interference.

Democracy:

Freedom of a *society* and each person in it in choosing and/or being rid of its government.

Sovereignty:

Freedom of a *government* to serve its people without external control or interference.

The United Kingdom is different from its Continental Europe neighbours, and as they say in France: *Vive la difference!*

But <u>why</u> are *Anglosphere values and norms* different?

The following reasons are offered:

1. The UK is an *island nation* and its whole psyche is therefore different from that of its Continental Europe neighbours.

2. It became a maritime power in the time of King Alfred the Great, first needing to defend itself from marauding forces across the seas, then seeking to know what was on the other side of the world, then seeking trade and a need to defend that trade. This influenced *a global, outward view.*

3. The UK is a nation made up of people from around the world coming for economic freedom, freedom of religion, freedom from political persecution and racism, and for quality of life.

4. It has a sense of *nationhood and monarchy* going back a thousand years, compared with its European neighbours, which typically date from the 1800s.

5. Its *system of law* is based on: (a) common law pre-dating Magna Carta in 1215, (b) legislative law from the oldest, national parliament, (c) case law based on precedent, and (d) the principle that you have the freedom to do anything provided there is no law against it.

6. It is a "Nation of Shop-Keepers", as Napoleon Bonaparte called the UK – meant as a slur but taken as a compliment to its *culture of trade and entrepreneurial spirit.*

7. Free trade, like free enterprise, and like democracy itself, is not without its downside – yet *free trade is a principle held dear.*

8. In the late 1600s shipping insurance and stock and commodity prices were provided in London coffee houses.

   Since then the UK has developed into a global centre offering financial and consultancy services to the world, such that *financial and consulting expertise* are now part of the UK's DNA.

9. It's the home of *team sports, playing by the rules, and fair play* in football, rugby, cricket, hockey, netball, tennis, curling, polo, etc.

10. It's the home of *rich and diverse humour*, with comedians and comedies too numerous to mention.

Anglosphere values and norms (of the English-speaking world) – have been hard-won going back to before Magna Carta in 1215, and they continue to be hard-won today.

This might be compared with the way the EU does things, and the question asked:

How many Anglosphere values and norms are the same, or different, from the way the EU does things?

This is not saying that Anglosphere governments are always true to these values and norms.

They're assessed as being the same, different, or the comparison not applicable, as shown in the following list:

✓   The same.
X   Different.
n.a. Not applicable

These notations are placed *before* each value/norm.

Liberty

X The pre-eminence of the Individual above The State: the individual person has inalienable and natural rights which are generally above those of The State.

X Liberty and freedom of action is generally unrestricted unless there is a law which controls or prohibits it.

X The universal right of trial by jury in criminal cases, by fellow citizens, in which unanimous verdict is required.

X Freedom of speech (provided there is no serious harm or threat intended for anyone).

X Freedom of belief and religion, without state-imposed 'political correctness'.

X Freedom of the press, albeit with ethical responsibility.

✓ Freedom of assembly and meeting.

n.a. Freedom of expression in the arts.

X Freedom, if not encouragement, to start and grow a business without undue government interference.

Liberty

X Freedom from arbitrary/undue state/government prejudice, interference, or intrusion (incl. privacy and *data* privacy).

✓ Land and property rights secure and protected by law.

X An expectation of truth, fairness, and 'playing by the rules'.

X A system of case law based on 'bottom-up' precedent, versus the 'top-down' form in the Napoleonic *Code Civil*, which is the basis of law in much of Continental Europe.

X Respect for the law: "The Law of the Land" – *legem terrae*.

X Freedom from arbitrary arrest (the writ of *habeas corpus*), detention, and/or cruel treatment in policing/justice.

X The presumption of innocence in policing/justice.

X Cannot be tried for the same crime twice (double jeopardy).

X Legal issues and disputes arbitrated by independent judges or magistrates exercising their role without bias.

Democracy

The word "democracy" or "democratic" means <u>of the demos,</u> of the <u>people</u>, and it is not used or seen in the same way around the world, as for example in the Democratic People's Republic of Korea (North Korea), and the former German Democratic Republic (Communist East Germany).

Nor does it mean the same thing from the European Union perspective as it does for Anglosphere countries.

X It is the will of the people that makes the law.

X Government has the authority to collect taxes from its citizens and is accountable for how their tax money is spent.

X Bicameral upper/lower legislatures for the initiation, review, and enactment of laws.

✓ Voting choice among distinct parties and/or independents.

X An expectation of ethical behaviour and freedom from corruption and self-serving in politicians and public officials.

X Law-making government clearly and directly accountable on a regular basis to the people through the ballot box.

X The law cannot be changed by executive power or officialdom except in time of war or national emergency.

Democracy

X No-one is above the law.

X Government governs with the consent of the people,
   and laws are not passed without mandate of the people.

✓ One person one vote, with free and secret voting.

X Government decision-making processes to follows as
   feasible the 'fishbowl' principle of being transparent.

X The executive arm of government (the P.M./cabinet arm)
   answerable to the legislative/parliamentary arm.

X The executive arm of government comprised of people
   elected by the people.

X Parliament directly answerable to the people, and
   responsible for controlling excessive power in the executive
   arm of government.

X Government decisions taken as closely as possible
   to the people they affect (subsidiarity).

Sovereignty (self-governance)

A government:

X is itself responsible for the defence of the country against exterior threat, inimical influence, and/or assault on the nation's critical needs and interests.

X never willingly abandons or shares the nation's sovereignty to/with any other authority or power it cannot influence or control.

X is responsible for putting its own citizens and their interests first, before the citizens of any and all other countries.

X has power to legislate and govern without interference or intrusion by any other state or power.

X is responsible for promoting peace, understanding, and the resolution of inter-governmental concerns on behalf of and according to the will of its own citizens.

PART III: KEY QUESTIONS

- Would the UK be more successful outside the EU?

- Would we still be able to live/work/study/retire in the EU?

- What would be involved in moving out of the EU?

.

There are good reasons why we can feel confident that the UK can more than survive outside the EU.

1. The UK has something like the fifth or sixth biggest economy in the world. According to the Office of National Statistics (ONS) it continued to grow in the last quarter of 2015, and the UK economy is one of the fastest growing among developed nations. The International Monetary Fund (IMF) has forecasted continued growth.

2. The City is one of the top global, financial services centres, and it can continue to be if it does not have the excessive, legislative over-kill and bureaucracy of the European Union. It was said that the City would die if we did not join the Eurozone; instead it did even better. It is now said the City will die if we leave the EU; but again there is every reason to believe it will do better.

3. Outside the EU the UK would have the freedom to negotiate out own FTAs, which would enable us to play to our strengths and market UK brands (See the section on *The UK: An FTA hub*)

4. At one time the United Kingdom was workshop to the world, a global leader in manufacturing quality products. *British is Best* was not just a cliché. With its increasing attraction for foreign direct investment (FDI) it looks like it may now, once again, become a centre for top-end manufacturing with its strengths in pharmaceuticals, biotechnology, agri-food, aerospace, car production, and advanced engineering.

5. The UK (according to *Media Week*), is the world's leading e-commerce exporter, ahead of the United States and Germany.

6. And we have, for a long time, been a great trading nation; it's part of our DNA.

7. Five of our universities are in the global top ten and, in what is not just an *Information Society* but a global

Knowledge Economy, this has to be considered a critical success factor.

8. The IT software industry is second only to that of the United States.

9. UK art, design, fashion & style, music, TV programmes, and films/movies are exported around the world.

10. UK companies have many quality, global brands known and accepted around the world, such as Burberry, Brompton Bikes, Rolls Royce, Aston Martin, Dr Martens, BBC, ITV, Prudential, Next, Asos, Jaeger, Mulberry, Russell & Bromley, Barbour, Next, Jimmy Choo, HSBC, Barclays, BAE Systems, Thomson Reuters, M&S, Waitrose, BP, Vodaphone, Shell, Dyson, Jaguar, Land Rover, Rio Tinto, Virgin Media, Sky, British Airways, Deloitte, PWC, Unilever, RBS, GlaxoSmithKline . . . and anything of which the Duchess of Cambridge is seen to approve.

11. We belong to the 50-plus family of nations in the Commonwealth, including India, Sri Lanka, Pakistan, Nigeria, Australia, New Zealand, Canada, South Africa, Singapore, Cyprus, Jamaica, and other advanced or rapidly growing economies. These and other Commonwealth countries offer a massive opportunity for FTAs.

12. We have a very good diplomatic and trading relationship with the United States, which would be even better outside of the EU, very likely with a FTA.

13. St Andrews is the home of golf; Wembley is the home of football; Twickenham is the home of rugby; Wimbledon is the home of tennis; Lords is the home of cricket; Henley is the home of rowing; Silverstone is the home of Formula 1. They all attract financial investment, visitors, and attention to the United Kingdom and what it has to offer.

14. Many parents around the world send their children to be educated in UK schools and universities; an invisible and generally under-appreciated strength.

15. The UK is a maritime and military power, clearly not what it used to be but still with a lot of clout and a globally respected military tradition.

16. English is the language that everyone wants to learn.

17. Heathrow/Gatwick provide an excellent, global-reach, air travel hub.

With these and other strengths there seems little doubt that the UK would become unshackled, able to achieve its true potential, and more successful outside of the European Union.

Would we still be able to live/work/study/retire in the EU?

There are said to be about two million UK citizens living in EU member countries. About half are retired and half are working. The most popular country is Spain, followed by France and Ireland.

The following criteria are used for anyone applying for residency in the United Kingdom, and it's very likely that largely similar, quid pro quo criteria, would apply for UK citizens wishing to live, work, study, or retire in an EU country - if the UK votes to leave:

1. **UK ancestry.** You're a Commonwealth citizen and have a grandparent born in the UK or Ireland (and Irish citizens do not need their EU connection to live in the UK; the right to reside and vote goes back long before the EEC/EU).

2. **Family Visa.** You have a parent or spouse who is a UK citizen.

3. **Skilled Worker.** Applies if you have a job offer, and you can apply to remain in the UK based on a factors such as previous earnings, professional qualifications, and age.

4. **Wealth/Investor Visa.** You can show that you have a minimum of two million pounds available to invest in the UK, in shares, bonds, or a direct business investment - made within three months. The more invested the better and easier it is to enter on this visa, it's good for three years, and can be extended for another two, after which you can apply for permanent residency.

5. **Entrepreneur Visa.** You have a minimum of £200,000 to invest and can prove you have a long-term commitment to take on at least two employees.

6. **Study Visa.** For a course of study at an accredited institution, after which you have four months to find a job and remain in the UK.

7. **Youth mobility Scheme.** This is for two years residency and is for people from 18 to 30 who have at least £2,000 in savings. After this you can apply for a study visa.

It must be said that, if the UK leaves the EU, then European travel would not be as easy, especially at peak times. Except that, as biometric UK passports become more common, it will become easier compared to paper bound, visual recognition passports.

And if, for example, you have family already living in an EU country; or are a skilled worker already having a job or a job to go to; or have money to invest; or applying to study; or wish to reside as a youth for a period - then it's very likely you would be able to live/work/study/retire in the EU, as before.

And if you're already resident or have property in an EU country such as Spain, Portugal, or France (and of course Ireland), then your status would remain unchanged. It's known as an "executed right" under Article 70b of the Vienna Convention. There is also the well-recognised principle of acquired (vested) rights.

There are also a couple of practical reasons for this:

1. It would not be diplomatically acceptable to require you to leave, and

2. your money and your spending would be needed for jobs and the economy of that country.

As for studying in an EU country, there are many schemes around the world for the exchange of students and academics. Individual institutions even have their own schemes. This has been encouraged for a very long time, long before the EEC/EU, because the exchange of knowledge and learning is internationally recognised and well accepted. It will continue whether the UK remains in or leaves the EU, and this would include the EU Erasmus scheme.

So, no big changes.

Prepared plans

This section aims to hit the key points on *what needs to be done* in leaving the EU.

It would seem very unlikely that the UK Government would *not* have a prepared plan ready, if the Referendum vote is to leave the EU.

But even if there is no Government Plan, there are other plans in place, notably:

- The plan prepared by Iain Mansfield (Director of Trade & Investment at the UK Philippines Embassy), titled *A Blueprint for Britain*, which won the £100,000 prize for best submission awarded by the institute of Economic Affairs. Mr Mansfield has since been banned by the UK Government from speaking in the EU In or Out debate.

- The 400-page plan prepared by Dr Richard North (co-author of *The Great Deception*) and Mr Robert Oulds (author of *Everything You Wanted to Know About the EU – But Were Afraid to Ask)*. The plan is titled *Flexcit: The Definitive EU Exit Plan for Britain*.

So that leaving the EU would not be a "leap into the dark" as some have said.

Setting the scene

If the UK votes to leave the EU a two-year negotiation process will be required with the EU. The procedure is in Article 50 of the 2002 Lisbon Treaty.

And in articles 3, 8, and 50 of the Lisbon Treaty, the EU is *constitutionally required* to negotiate "free and fair trade" with non-EU countries – which the UK would become.

Also, the World Trade Organisation (of which the EU is a member on behalf of its 28 member countries) – makes it illegal to discriminate against exports/imports to/from non-EU countries – including the UK.

This means that it is highly unlikely there would be any reproach, recrimination, or reprisal from the EU if the UK votes to leave the EU.

If there were, we could either: (a) invoke the EU and WTO articles against discrimination or (b) walk away from the negotiations, and deal with the EU in the same way that any other country without a FTA with the EU operates (such as the United States, a very big exporter into the EU Single Market).

The advantage in the case of (b) would be that the UK would be free of the heavy cost and burden of EU regulations, and free of the protective import tariffs that the EU imposes on imports to any EU country from outside the EU.

However, since there would be mutual gain in a UK/EU FTA, this is by far the most likely scenario. In the end, people and countries do what's in their best interests.

Main Tasks to be Done

The EU Leaving Process would have a number of main tasks:

- Immediately begin negotiations for free trade agreements (FTAs), with countries and areas such as the United States, India, Canada, Japan, China, Australia, New Zealand, South Korea, Switzerland, Norway, Turkey, Chile, Israel, Egypt, Central America, South Africa, West Africa, East Africa, and the Gulf States

A lot of people would need to be put to this task – or set of tasks - some of whom (a) could be brought and bought in who have experience in this area, as for example the Swiss, and (b) UK civil servants presently tasked with EU-related jobs who could be re-trained, first, in supporting negotiation, and second, promoting UK trade around the world in restored UK trade roles.

- Negotiate a FTA with the EU, to be joined to but separate from the leaving process.

- Pass an act of Parliament to repeal the 1972 European Communities Act (which got us into the EEC), which would need to include "any provisions of the European Communities Act notwithstanding".

- Develop an Immigration Policy based on a points system, similar to Australia, New Zealand, and the United States.

- Reclaim the UK's fishing grounds, through international legal processes as required, as per The United Nations Law of the Sea of 1994, which recognises Exclusive Economic Zones and gives countries exclusive fishing zones up to 200 miles from their shore lines or the median point between countries.

- Develop a UK Fisheries Policy for sensible and agile governance of the UK's restored fishing grounds, in a complete break from the present EU CFP, and learning from its mistakes.

- Develop a UK Agricultural Policy for sensible and streamlined governance of the UK's farming, in a complete break from the present EU CAP, and with consideration for farmer viability.

- Assess and resolve the legal aspects of EU regulations and directives that have become part of UK Justice & Home Affairs, especially the European Arrest Warrant. Also, the restoration of UK passports and driving licenses.

- Make a cost assessment of the most burdensome and costly EU regulations, to determine which should be prioritised for cancelling or phasing out, such as the Large Combustion Plant Directive, the Temporary Agency Workers Directive, the Alternative Investment Fund Managers Directive, and the Climate Change Act.

- Assess energy policy and climate change targets so as to remove current EU complexity and cost, with a view to reducing green levies and the cost of gas and electricity for consumers.

- Undertake a process for cancelling or phasing out EU regulations, as for example the Working Time Directive, to include a question along the following lines:

  Is this EU regulation needed for the UK and therefore something to be retained?

  If so, why is it needed, and how could it be made more efficient & effective?

  If not, then how can it best and most fairly be phased out?

- Codify the transitional arrangements for (a) citizens in the other 27 EU countries presently living in the UK, and (b) UK citizens living in the other EU countries.

- Removal of all mention of the UK from EU treaties.

- Restore the primacy of UK courts, as against the European Court of Justice.

- Assess the position of the City and how it should be best positioned and protected from present and future EU regulations.

There is no doubt that other main tasks would be involved, and a more detailed and comprehensive list can be gained from the two EU exit plans cited at the beginning of this section.

SOURCES

Abula, David, editor, with Nigel Saul, Robert Tombs, Andrew Roberts, Edward Hicks, Sheila Lawlor, and Oliver Davis.
European Demos: A Historical Myth? 2015.
The answer to the question by this group of historians is: yes it is a myth. There is no European *demos* or 'people'. There is no common sense of a European political or social identity, nor has there ever been. On the other hand there is a history of UK/Europe history going back many centuries, the 1373 alliance with Portugal being an example. This is a fascinating and enjoyable read for anyone interested in the history of Europe.

Ambler, Tim, Chitenden, Francis, and Bashir, Asif.
Counting the Cost of EU Regulation on Business. 2009.
This study/report by senior academics from London Business School and Manchester Business School was prepared for *Eurochambres*, which is the European association of Chambers of Commerce. Its headline is that the cost to business of EU regulations represents a "significant percentage of EU GDP".

Bank of England.
EU Membership and the Bank of England. 2015.
A one hundred page report accompanying Governor Mark Carney's 21 October 2015 speech to the City of London Corporation and Open Europe Conference at Oxford University. Provides useful information on the UK's position in global markets and the EU-wide regulatory response to the 2008 financial markets crisis. It says that free flow of capital is both opportunity and threat – hence the need for a common regulatory regime.

bbc.co.uk/news
The BBC News web site has been a most useful source of information in undertaking the research and keeping up to date for this book. Thankfully and to its credit (and although it has been biased in the past), this time around it has been reasonably non-biased on the EU In or Out Question, with special credit particularly to the new Political Editor, Laura Kuenssberg.

Bidelaux, Robert, and Taylor, Richard.
European Integration and Disintegration. 1996.

A collection of essays by academic writers, taking a broad and historical view, providing useful background on political Europe.

Bootle, Roger.
The Trouble with Europe. 2014.
A balanced analysis by this leading, prize-winning economist; full of practical wisdom and insight.

Booker, Christopher, and North, Richard.
The Great Deception: Can the European Union Survive? 2005.
This book demonstrates that you cannot understand the present without knowing the past. With painstaking analysis and logic it uncovers the history behind the European project using a vast volume of original source material, memoirs, and official government records. It shows that the same stories repeat themselves again and again. With more than 600 pages and hundreds of footnotes this book is not an easy read, but for anyone wanting to know the real history behind the European Union and understand it today, it's a compelling eye-opener and page-turner.

Britain Stronger in Europe. Strongerin.co.uk
A group and web site arguing the case for EU-In, on the basis that the UK is stronger, better off, and safer in Europe than it would be on its own, with more jobs and opportunities.

Business for Britain. businessforbritain.org.uk
Change or Go: How Britain Would Gain Influence and Prosper Outside an Unreformed EU. 2015.
A very comprehensive and factual analysis of the whole EU In/Out issue including, for example, the EU impact on the cost of living for households. The conclusion is that the UK might still be able to get true EU reform but if not – then we must leave.

Centre for European Reform. cer.org.uk
The Five Presidents' Report: An Assessment. 2015.
This report by Christian Odendahl shows where the EU falls short of effective action for reform.

Charter, David.
Europe: In or Out: Everything You Need to Know. 2014.

A well-balanced, factual, informative, and easy to read analysis of the whole EU In/Out issue.

Chitanden, Francis, Ambler, Tim, and Bashir, Asif.
Counting the Cost of EU Regulation to Business. 2009.
This report was prepared for Eurochambres, which is the European Association of Chambers of Commerce and industry, representing the view of businesses large and small across the EU. It is diplomatically critical of the excessive cost of EU regulation and bureaucracy, and is one of the several attempts to estimate its cost. For the UK, as of the date of the report, it was about ten £billion. It is particularly critical of the way the EU gives little or no attention to the financial and practical impact of its regulatory measures and, in spite of promises to do something about this, never has.

City of London Corporation.
Where Next Europe: the Future of Financial Services. May, 2015.
The report highlights what the EU stands to gain by getting regulatory reform right, but expresses concern about too much EU regulation.

TheCityUK.com
A lobbying group that champions UK-based financial and related professional services. In favour of remaining in a reformed EU. The group's view is that UK membership of the EU is of strategic importance to the financial and related professional services industry, and works to bring about reform in (a) deepening the EU Single Market for financial services, and (b) so that the Banking Union, Capital Markets Union, and ever-closer Eurozone integration do not undermine the interests of non-Eurozone members. For these things to happen, reform is essential.

Civitas: The Institute for the Study of Civil Society
A think tank and educational charity. It provides balanced, concise, and plain-speaking research on key social issues in society, including for/against school worksheets on the EU.

Clarke, Stephen.
1000 Years of Annoying the French. 2010.

An enjoyable and amusing read, but with a serious undercurrent. The elephant in the room with the European Union is the age-old, love-hate relationship between France and the Anglosphere, and this book tells why.

Congdon, Tim
'Europe' doesn't Work: A discussion of the three-million-jobs-at-risk lie and related misconceptions. 2013.
Professor Tim Congdon shows why those three million job losses are a factoid, and gives a detailed and convincing analysis of how and why, since joining the European Union, the UK has experienced a loss of jobs.

Congdon, Tim.
The City of London in Retreat. 2014.
An analysis by this professor of economics of how the transfer of regulatory powers to the EU under the 2007 Lisbon Treaty could destroy the UK's financial services industry.

Congdon, Tim
How Much Does the European Union Cost Britain? 2014.
This 39-page booklet gives a concise summary of the direct and indirect costs of EU membership, particularly the impact costs of the 200,000-page *Aquis Communautaire* (the EU's body of law).

Connolly, Bernard.
The Rotten Heart of Europe. 2012.
A master lesson in practical macroeconomics, using the EU as a virtual case study, by this leading economist - who held a senior position in the EU Commission before he became whistle-blower. Commended by Bank of England Governor Mark Carney for his prescient insight.

Coughlan, Anthony.
The Nation State, Sovereignty, and the European Union.
Studies: An Irish Quarterly Review, Vol. 93, Issue 369, Spring 2004.
A senior academic from Trinity College, Dublin, discusses nine democratic principles and argues that the European Union is fundamentally undemocratic and cannot be democratised.

Dalberg, John E.E. (Lord Acton), ed. J. Rufus Fears.

Essays in the History of Liberty. 1985.
A reprint of essays by this 19th century scholar; a much-quoted and most insightful thinker on liberty and democracy.

Dixon, Hugo.
The In/Out Question: Why Britain Should Stay in the EU and Fight to Make it Better. 2014.
Probably the best-argued case for remaining in the EU. The author is a successful journalist, and skilful wording is his forte in minimising the bad and exaggerating the good in and for his case. There is also a use of selective facts. However, there is no rhetoric, trivia, or sloganeering; just the (selective) facts as seen from the EU-In perspective.

The Economist
Leaving the EU would hurt Britain – and would also deal a terrible blow to the West
27 February, 2016.
The Economist has, for a very long time, been pro-EU and in favour of the UK remaining in the EU. It could be expected that the article would reflect this. The article includes about 15 inaccuracies.

Emerson, Michael (ed).
Britain's Future in Europe. 2015.
EU-funded academics discuss the UK Government's report on *Balances of Competences Review*. Presents the academic view for remaining in the European Union.

EurActiv.com
A useful web site providing up to date, objective reporting with the aim of promoting visibility and transparency on EU news, policies, activities, and debates.

EUReferendum.com
A daily blog authored by Dr Richard North (co-author of *FLEXCIT: A Definitive EU Exit Plan for Britain*), and formerly a research director in the European Parliament). Dr North may well be the most knowledgeable expert on the whole, complex EU issue.

Ernst & Young: Mark Gregory (Chief Economist).
Special Report on UK Business Investment. 2015.

According to this report, and even with IMF projections of a fall in global business investment as a whole, investment in the UK continues to rise, and the future outlook for the UK remains positive. This outlook subsequently confirmed by the IMF.

European Commission, Directorate-General for Communication. *How the European Union Works.* 2015.
The EU view of the EU; a shop window overview of the agencies and other bodies that are involved in the European Union's work.

Financial Services Authority
A Brief Guide to the European Union and its Legislative Processes. 2011. Focuses mostly on the Financial governance of the EU, and provisions for European Systemic Risk following the 2008 global markets crisis.

The Foreign Policy Centre
Renegotiation, Reform, and Referendum: **Does Britain Have an EU Future?** Adam Hug, editor. 2014.
13 academics and politicians give their assessment of the issues surrounding the EU Referendum issues, in an attempt to put some reasoned analysis on an otherwise adversarial debate.

Green, David G.
The Demise of the Free State: Why British Democracy and the EU Don't Mix. 2014.
A short and punchy book of 121 pages, it summarises why and how democracy and UK sovereignty are eroded in the EU.

Hannan, Daniel (MEP).
Inventing Freedom: How the English-Speaking Peoples Made the Modern World. 2013.
A book for our time, revealing in readable, well-researched, and fascinating style how Anglosphere liberty and democracy have been so hard-won over a thousand years.

Hayek ,Frederick August.
The Road to Serfdom. 1944.
A classic; how liberty is easily lost, piece by piece, as The State intrudes in the name of expediency and necessity into the lives of its citizens. Also, the impossibility of effective, centralised,

government planning - and its generally terrible consequences whenever it has been tried.

Heaton-Harris, (MP), Chris, and Broadhurst, Robert (researcher)
European Scrutiny Submission of the House of Commons ESI 07. 2012.
Recommends how the Scrutiny Committee's working might be reformed, given: (a) the EU gives no role or status to national parliaments, yet (d) "produces vast quantities of legislation" and excessive workloads for them to consider, (b) the committee has only a junior status and has minimal influence on government policy, (c) its rotating membership, the few MPs involved, and their inability to build up EU knowledge, (d) the reluctance of MPs to serve on it, given the poor recognition and publicity in doing so, and given that the European Commission can ignore a parliament's recommendations. The report recommends the Danish model be adopted.

Helmer, Roger (MEP).
A Declaration of Independence. 2002.
An inside story on the EU's bureaucracy, waste, and democracy deficit. Passionately in favour of leaving the EU.

Hindley, Brian, and Howe, Martin.
Better Off Out? The Benefits or Costs of EU Membership. 2001.
This publication from the Institute of Economic Affairs by a professor specialising in trade policy and a QC who conducts cases before English courts and the European Court of Justice, may seem out of date by now, but its insights are not. Their conclusion is that leaving the EU would have, on balance, relatively little effect on the UK economy. However, they say, it would be foolish to make a decision on the basis of economic reasons alone.

House of Lords, European Union Committee.
The Review of Competences Between the UK and the EU. 2015.
Long-winded, and not much in the way of insights.

Jenkins, Lindsay

An investigative journalist with a deep and sharp knowledge of the European Union. She has an author page on Amazon, and her books are recommended.

Juncker, Jean-Claude (Pres. European Commission).
Completing Europe's Economic & Monetary Union,
commonly known as ***The Five Presidents' Report.*** 2015.
ec.europa.eu/priorities/economic monetary union/docs/5 presidents report.
A revealing and comprehensive statement of EU aims. Can be viewed as either (a) justifying the EU aim of complete political integration of all member countries into the EU, or (b) making clear why genuine change/reform in the EU (since it would back-track on this aim) is unlikely. It states the aim of complete political union in a United States of Europe by 2025.

Kemppinen, Reijo. (Head of the EU Commission Repr. In the UK)
The EU: What's In It for Me? Europe Direct. Un-dated.
An EU publication and EU shop window for UK citizens.

Kohr, Leopold.
The Breakdown of Nations. 1957.
This book is about the Problem of Bigness in government – for which the solution is de-centralisation, devolution, and genuine subsidiarity. There will always be problems, but with big government they are *big* problems, the book says. And it certainly seems to be the case that people in smaller states are happier, have a greater sense of identity with and sovereignty in their government, are able to get things done more efficiently and effectively, and enjoy greater prosperity and sense of freedom.

Christoffer Kølvraa
European Fantasies: On the EU's Political Myths and the Affective Potential of Utopian Imaginaries for European Identity.
Journal of Common Market Studies. 2016, vol. 54, issue 1, pages 169-184
An academic perspective on the problem of disenchantment with the European political project, arguing that the political myth involves the utopian dream of peace and understanding, and suggests that the disenchantment might be partly due to the dream having been achieved.

Kovach, Bill and Rosenstiel, Tom.
Blur: How to Know What's True in the Age of Information Overload. 2011.
A book by these veteran journalists on how to use active scepticism in what you read in the media; particularly useful in separating the wheat from the chaff in media reporting on the run-up to the EU Referendum.

Kreijen, Gerard, Brus, Marcel, Duursma, Jorris, De Vos, Elizabeth, and Dugard, John.
State, Sovereignty, and International Governance. 2002.
This series of academic essays deals with the issue of supra-national bodies and their potential impact in diminishing the role of sovereign states. On the one hand you have the aspirations of people and the fundamental human value of being sovereign and self-governing. On the other hand there is a the need for national governments to co-operate effectively for the resolution of global problems. All of the contributors agree that sovereignty of the nation state is paramount. But they also agree that sovereignty cannot be isolated from the need to address the concerns of the international community.

Lea, Ruth, and Binley, Brian (MP).
Britain and Europe: A New Relationship. 2012.
This lengthy paper is by an economist with extensive experience in advising government and banks, and an MP responsible for business innovation and skills. It deals with the three million job losses myth, and estimates that the cost of the EU Single Market for the UK outweighs the benefits by about 2.5:1. Overall, it says the cost of EU membership for the UK is "unequivocally negative". It also shows why the UK should leave the EU if the City is to survive.

Leach, Rodney.
Europe: A Concise Encyclopedia of the European Union. 2004.
The book's Introduction begins with "It is not only to the amateur that the EU is confusing" – and then goes on to give material help in reducing that confusion with a vast array of facts and well-written explanatory comment. Its description of the "European Idea" is the best summing-up of the European .

LeGrain ,Philippe.
European Spring: Why Our Economies and Politics are in a Mess and How to Put Them Right. 2014.
Former advisor to Pres. Barroso of the European Commission. A sympathetic account of where the EU has gone wrong,

Liberal Democrat Voice. www.libdemvoice.org
As the name clearly says, a web site giving the Liberal Democrat view of the world. Very much *EU-In.*

Liddle, Roger.
The Europe Dilemma: The Trouble with Europe. 2014.
A former aide to Tony Blair and close to Gordon Brown. Calls for the UK to adopt the Euro. Passionately in favour of remaining in the EU.

Lindsell, Jonathan.
Lessons from Switzerland: How might Britain go about business outside the EU? 2015.
This book shows that a small county can do very well in cutting trade deals, as for example Switzerland did with Japan, one of the world's biggest economies. If the Swiss can do it so well with a much smaller country there seems no reason why the UK cannot.

Middlemas, Keith.
Orchestrating Europe: The Informal Politics of the European Union 1973-1993. 1995.
Out of date yet with significant implications: how P.M. Margaret Thatcher was outmanoeuvred by EU leaders Bettino Craxi and Giulio Andreotti.

Minford, Patrick, Gupta, Sakshi, Vo Phuong Mai Lee, Vidia Mahuambare, and Yongdeng Xu.
Should Britain Leave the EU? An Economic Analysis of a Troubled Relationship. (Second edition) 2015.
The key contributions that Professor Minford and his colleagues give us in this book are: (1) the way it unwraps important economic assumptions about the EU Single Market and the impact of its regulatory compliance (which is easily the biggest of EU costs for member states), (2) the cost of EU protectionism against products from outside the EU (also a big cost in the

outcome of higher prices in the shops), and (3) the macroeconomics of international trade (in which it's shown that there is likely to be a significant boost to exports if the UK is outside the EU and free to negotiate its own free trade agreements). The book also argues that if the UK remains part of the EU: (4) the EU doctrine of ever-closer union will mean increasing pressure to join the Eurozone, and (5) the City will always be at the mercy of majority voting, which will be against UK interests and the City's EU-perceived "unfair competitive advantage". This is an enlightening book.

Money Week
Merryn Somerset Webb. Editor-in-Chief.
A magazine directed mainly at investors, but of interest for many, covering the area of money (how to invest it, spend it, and keep it), finance, economics, and politics in an entertaining way and, most importantly, packing as much useful information as possible into the least number of words, making it easier to understand and time-efficient in getting useful information.

Morisi, Paoli.
The Role of Christian Democracy in Support of European Integration.
Studies: An Irish Quarterly Review, Vol. 93, Issue 369, Spring 2004.
Argues for European integration as the aim of Christian Democratic parties in avoiding war and conflict.

North, Richard E. and Oulds, Robert
Flexcit: the definitive EU exit plan for Britain. 2015.
With over 400 pages by these leading experts on the European Union, this has to be the definitive version of what the UK should do and how it should go about it if the vote is to leave the EU.

www.nouvelle-europe.eu
A French-based web site having partnerships with the ESSC Business School and the University of the Sorbonne Nouvelle, and the EU itself. It is largely oriented to promoting EU causes to young people. Its useful articles give an understanding of the French view.

Open Europe. openeurope.org.uk

What If? The Consequences, Challenges, and Opportunities Facing Britain Outside the EU. 2015.
Economic projections to 2030. Shows there would be little economic difference whether the UK remains in or leaves the EU.

Open Europe (Authors Raoul Ruparel and Stephen Booth).
A Blueprint for Reform of the European Union. June, 2015.
A well-balanced and thoughtful analysis which has a number of similarities to P.M. Cameron's 10 Nov. Proposals to Donald Tusk (President of the European Council). However, Open Europe is not truly independent: (1) it's in favour of remaining in the EU albeit with fundamental reforms and based on the Single Market, and (2) it assumes that reform is realistically possible.

Oulds, Robert.
Everything You Wanted to Know About the EU – But Were Afraid to Ask. 2013.
This book is true to its title. A very useful in-depth, scholarly work giving real insight into the inner workings of the EU, the nature of the EU, and its impact on the economic and social fabric of society, using sources not generally available. It packs lot of facts into a page-turning narrative of just 200 pages. The number of real experts on the EU could be counted on the fingers of two hands, and this book shows the author to be one of them.

Parkinson, C. Northcote.
Parkinson's Law: The Pursuit of Progress. 2002.
Originally published by Houghton Mifflin 1956, later published as a Penguin Classic, 2002. This is the classic work on bureaucracy and make-work in government, especially big government.

Pinder, John, and Usherwood, Simon.
The European Union: A Very Short Introduction. 2013.
A good introduction to the EU but not, as the authors claim, a scrupulously balanced book. It's assumptions clearly put it on the side of *EU-In*, the only question being whether the EU should be more or less federalist and integrationist.

The Pink Book www.ons.gov.uk
This is the official book of the Office for National Statistics (ONS), in which can be found figures for trade with the EU and the Rest of the World.

Pisani-Ferry, Jean.
The Euro Crisis and Its Aftermath. 2011.
A historical analysis of where the EU has gone wrong and what is
needed to put it right for a future world economy.

Proeuropa.org.uk
A passionately pro-EU web site with several close ties to the EU.
It articulates _Reasons to Stay_ in the EU, the first of which focuses
on the EU Single Market and 3.5 million British jobs directly linked
to UK EU membership.

Pycock, Daniel C.
The plan to leave the European Union _by 2020._ 2015
Daniel was a finalist in the Institute of Economic Affair's
competition for papers to outline a UK plan for 'Brexit'. It covers
the constitutional process, the impact on trade, the City of London
and financial services, Fiscal Policy, and Immigration. It is well-
supported by statistical analysis. This is a plan that needs to be
looked at by the UK government if the UK votes to leave.

Rowthorn, Robert.
The Costs and Benefits of Large-Scale Immigration:
Exploring the Economic and Demographic Consequences for
the UK. 2015.
A timely and well-balanced book by a distinguished economist,
looking at both the hard and soft cost v. benefit issues of the
immigration debate.

Schumacher, Ernst F.
Small is Beautiful: A Study of Economics as if People
Mattered. 1993.
A classic; not just people but the environment as well. Explains
the _subsidiarity_ principle of devolved government. The chapter on
A Question of Size helps to explain why 'Big is Good' is a fallacy.
It's a book that needs to be kept on the shelf and read more than
once to challenge if not rid ourselves of some economic
'chestnuts'.

Stewart, Ewen.
Britain's Global Leadership. 2015.

A point-by-point reminder of the diversity and many strength areas of the UK as one of the world's strongest economies.

Springford, John, and Tilford, Simon.
Centre for European Reform
The Great British Trade-Off: The Impact of Leaving the EU on the UK's Trade and Investment. 2014.
The authors work for the Centre for European Reform, (CER), which is a think tank committed to remaining in the EU largely based on the EU Single Market, albeit with hoped-for EU reform. This is a well-argued case using a statistical technique called *fixed effects.* It compares EU trade with the UK versus non-EU trade, and concludes that the benefits of remaining in the EU outweigh the costs of leaving. However, it has an important *non sequitur.* that the UK accounts for only 10% of other EU member countries exports as a whole, compared to the EU, which is said to account for 45% of UK exports. For this reason, the UK would not have a strong bargaining advantage in negotiating exit terms with the EU. But this fails to compare like with like: the EU is much bigger than the UK, and 10% of its exports going to the UK is a very large volume lot of exports. The authors also assume that EU reform is possible which, for anyone familiar with the history, culture, the way the EU works, and body of law in the A*cquis Communautaire,* could be seen as extremely unlikely.

StrongerIn.co.uk
The EU-In web site of the campaign by the same name, led by Stuart Rose, former chairman of M&S. It argues that remaining in the EU would make the UK economically stronger and more secure, while leaving would cost many jobs. It assumes it to be unlikely that a favourable free trade agreement (FTA) could be struck with the EU, if the UK were to leave.

UKandEU.ac.uk
An independent and useful web and blog site with short article contributions by academics who are specialists in politics, law, foreign affairs, public policy, migration, social policy, and macroeconomics. It is refreshingly non-biased and neutral.

ABOUT THE AUTHOR

Dr C. James Bacon (PhD) studied for an MSc in Monetary Economics at the London School of Economics, then gained a Diploma in method/work study and worked in the City of London as a business process and efficiency consultant.

He later moved into systems consulting on Wall Street, New York, at the same time earning a part-time masters degree in strategic management (with honours) from NYU.

He then took up a position as Senior Lecturer in Information Management at the University of Canterbury in New Zealand, earning a doctorate and published articles in top, international journals.

In 1997 James and his wife Carmel moved back to England, where he taught at Bath University School of Management.

In early 2015, after finding that there were few sources that (a) provide a balanced view of both sides of the EU in or out question, and (b) provide it with concise, easy-to-use information, he began an intensive study of the question. This book is the result.